BON APPÉTIT®

Appetizers & Hors d'Oeuvres

THE CONDÉ NAST PUBLICATIONS INC.

Appetizers &
Hors d'Oeuvres

Introduction

If you scan the recipe index in any issue of *Bon Appétit*, you'll find listed there a generous helping of recipes under such headings as "Appetizers," "Salads," "Soups" and "Pasta." The reason we include so many is quite simple: Whether you are entertaining in gala fashion or just cooking a weekday dinner for the family, a good first impression makes any meal more special. That is why we take pride in offering you this complimentary collection of more than 120 great appetizer and hors d'oeuvre recipes taken from the pages of the magazine.

Strictly speaking, "appetizer" and "hors d'oeuvre" mean different things, even though the two terms have evolved to cover the same general range of foods.

An appetizer, as the word implies, whets the appetite for the courses that follow it. True appetizers are part of the menu, presented as first courses on individual plates to guests seated at the table.

The French term hors d'oeuvre, by contrast, translates literally as "outside the main work." In other words, hors d'oeuvres are meant to be served before or apart from a formal menu. They are bite-sized morsels–finger foods, if you will–designed to be passed around and enjoyed with cocktails or aperitifs, whether or not a sit-down meal is intended to follow.

As the different aspects of this book's title imply, the recipes on the pages that follow have been selected with versatility in mind. On the most basic level, you can leaf through them in search of new or unusual first courses to liven up your daily menus. Always make your choice, of course, with an eye toward complementing or contrasting pleasantly with the dishes to follow.

Alternatively, let this book be your one-stop source for planning a cocktail party menu. Just be sure to give some thought to providing a wide but compatible range of tastes and textures. And don't forget to select recipes than can be partially or completely made ahead, to give you ample time to enjoy your party as much as your guests will.

i

Bon Appétit®

Appetizers & Hors d'Oeuvres

CONTENTS

Dips & Spreads

Whether you scoop them up with vegetables or potato chips, or spread them on crackers or toast, the recipes that follow delight with luscious textures and rich, savory flavors. Ranging from lowfat Creamy Oregano Dip to indulgent Brie, Roquefort and Wild Mushroom fondue, and from piquant Green Olive Spread to mellow Smoked Fish Pâté, they have a power to please that is only exceeded by the speed of their preparation.

Dips

SPINACH AND GARLIC DIP WITH PITA TRIANGLES AND VEGETABLES

Fresh spinach, sautéed in oil with garlic, is pureed with sour cream and green onions to create this delicious dip.

6 SERVINGS

1½ teaspoons plus 2 tablespoons olive oil
2 teaspoons finely chopped garlic
8 cups (packed) fresh spinach leaves (about 5 ounces)

½ cup chopped green onions
1 cup sour cream
1 teaspoon fresh lemon juice

2 6-inch-diameter pita breads

Assorted raw vegetables

Heat 1½ teaspoons oil in large nonstick skillet over medium-high heat. Add garlic; sauté 10 seconds. Add spinach; sauté until wilted and tender, about 2 minutes. Cool.

Puree spinach and green onions in processor. Transfer to medium bowl. Mix in sour cream and lemon juice. Season with salt and pepper. Cover and chill.

Preheat broiler. Slice each pita bread horizontally in half, forming 2 circles. Cut each circle into 4 triangles. Place triangles in single layer on baking sheet. Lightly brush pita triangles with 2 tablespoons oil. Sprinkle with pepper. Broil until golden, watching closely to avoid burning and moving triangles on baking sheet to brown evenly, about 2 minutes. Cool. *(Dip and pita triangles can be made 1 day ahead. Keep dip chilled. Store pita in airtight container.)*

Serve dip with pita triangles and assorted raw vegetables.

GARLIC AND ANCHOVY DIP WITH VEGETABLES

This warm Italian dip of melted butter, olive oil, anchovies and garlic is usually accompanied by raw vegetables.

4 SERVINGS

1 cup extra-virgin olive oil
½ cup (1 stick) unsalted butter
8 canned anchovy fillets, chopped
3 garlic cloves, finely chopped
1 red bell pepper, cut into strips
1 yellow bell pepper, cut into strips
10 celery stalks, cut in half crosswise
6 green onions

Heat first 4 ingredients in heavy medium skillet over low heat until butter melts and mixture simmers, about 3 minutes. Season with salt and pepper. Transfer to flameproof bowl. Place over candle or canned heat burner. Serve with vegetables.

CREAMY OREGANO DIP WITH VEGETABLES

For this easy starter, the nonfat yogurt is strained to a thick texture and then combined with oregano, lemon peel and cayenne.

6 SERVINGS
(ABOUT 1¾ CUPS OF DIP)

3 cups plain nonfat yogurt

2 tablespoons chopped fresh
   oregano
½ teaspoon dried oregano
1 teaspoon grated lemon peel
1 teaspoon fresh lemon juice
½ teaspoon salt
½ teaspoon pepper
⅛ teaspoon cayenne pepper

2 heads Belgian endive, separated
   into spears
1 12-ounce basket cherry tomatoes

Set strainer over 4-cup measuring cup. Line strainer with paper towel. Add yogurt to strainer; chill until yogurt is thick (about 1 cup liquid will drain from yogurt), at least 2 hours or overnight.

Turn yogurt out into medium bowl; discard paper towel and drained liquid. Add chopped fresh and dried oregano, lemon peel, lemon juice, salt, pepper and cayenne to yogurt and stir to blend. Cover and refrigerate to develop flavors, at least 2 hours and up to 6 hours.

Place bowl with dip on platter. Surround with endive spears and cherry tomatoes and serve.

CRUDITÉS WITH BASIL AIOLI

A classic starter in Provence is assorted vegetables teamed with some aioli (garlic mayonnaise) for dipping. Basil is added to the mayonnaise for a nice variation.

6 SERVINGS

1 cup light mayonnaise
2 tablespoons olive oil
½ cup chopped fresh basil
4 garlic cloves, minced
⅛ teaspoon dried crushed red pepper

1 bunch radishes with leaves
1 green bell pepper, sliced
1 yellow bell pepper, sliced
1 bunch baby carrots, peeled
2 heads Belgian endive, each cut
   lengthwise into 6 wedges

Combine mayonnaise, 1 tablespoon oil and basil in medium bowl. Heat 1 tablespoon oil in heavy small skillet over medium-low heat. Add garlic and sauté until beginning to color, about 2 minutes. Add dried red pepper and sauté 30 seconds. Add to mayonnaise. Season with pepper. (*Can be made 1 day ahead. Cover; chill.*)

Serve vegetables with aioli.

LIGHT AND CREAMY GUACAMOLE

Plain nonfat yogurt heightens the texture of this easy dip while adding a nice tang. To thicken the yogurt properly, it needs to be drained, so begin preparing the guacamole at least two hours ahead.

MAKES ABOUT 1¾ CUPS

1½ cups plain nonfat yogurt

1 large ripe avocado, peeled, pitted, diced
¼ cup chopped green onions
¼ cup chopped fresh cilantro
1 teaspoon fresh lemon juice
¼ teaspoon ground cumin

3 carrots, peeled, sliced diagonally
1 small jicama, peeled, cut into ¼-inch-thick triangles
1 bunch radishes, trimmed, sliced
Fresh cilantro sprigs

Line strainer with double layer of cheesecloth. Set strainer over bowl. Add yogurt to strainer. Let drain in refrigerator until yogurt is very thick, at least 2 hours or overnight. Discard liquid.

Place yogurt in processor. Add avocado and next 4 ingredients to processor. Puree until smooth. Season with salt and pepper.

Transfer to bowl. (*Can be prepared 6 hours ahead. Cover and refrigerate.*)

Place guacamole in center of platter. Surround with carrots, jicama and radishes. Garnish with cilantro sprigs.

FAUX GUACAMOLE

Raw veggies are refreshing to eat during hot summer months, and nutritious treats at any time of year. But the high-fat and high-calorie dips they're often served with can sabotage these healthful snacks. Broccamole, from Mann Packing Company, is a fat-free, low-calorie dip made with delicious and good-for-you ingredients–and with no high-fat avocado. The creamy blend of nonfat mayonnaise, broccoli, tomatoes, garlic and mild green chilies has only ten calories in a two-tablespoon serving and is an excellent source of vitamin C. There is also a spicy variety, which is ideal for tacos, baked potatoes and baked tortilla chips. Broccamole is available in supermarkets.

BRIE, ROQUEFORT AND WILD MUSHROOM FONDUE

While fondue originated in the French-speaking part of Switzerland (the word means "melted" in French), the dish has become an international favorite. The principal ingredients are cheese (usually Gruyère mixed with either Emmenthal or Appenzeller), white wine, kirsch and garlic. But there are as many variations on that theme as there are mountains in Switzerland.

Custom decrees that anyone who loses a piece of bread in the hot cheese mixture–and it's not hard to do–supplies the guests with wine. The Swiss would suggest that it be the same one that is used in the fondue.

6 TO 8 SERVINGS

1½ teaspoons olive oil
4 ounces fresh shiitake mushrooms, stemmed, caps diced
1 shallot, minced
1 teaspoon chopped fresh thyme
1½ tablespoons all purpose flour
12 ounces chilled 60% (double crème) Brie cheese (do not use triple crème)
2 ounces chilled Roquefort cheese
1 cup dry white wine

1 13-ounce loaf crusty white bread, cut into 1½-inch cubes
Vegetables (such as carrot sticks, blanched broccoli, cauliflower and boiled small potatoes)

Heat oil in heavy medium skillet over medium-high heat. Add mushrooms, shallot and thyme; sauté until mushrooms just begin to soften, about 2 minutes.

Place flour in large bowl. Cut rind from Brie; discard rind. Cut Brie into cubes; drop into flour. Toss to coat; separate cheese cubes. Crumble Roquefort into same bowl; toss to coat. Place wine in heavy medium saucepan and bring to simmer over medium heat. Add cheese by handfuls, stirring until melted after each addition. Continue stirring until smooth.

Stir mushroom mixture into fondue. Season with generous amount of pepper. Transfer to fondue pot. Set pot over candle or canned heat burner. Serve with bread and vegetables.

FONDUE IS RED HOT

...and so is the sturdy French-made fondue set from Sisson Imports. The 2½-quart enameled cast-iron pot comes with a stand and 12 ten-inch forks. Call Cookworks at 800-972-3357.

HOT CRAB DIP WITH CRISP PITA WEDGES

12 SERVINGS

1 12-ounce package pita bread, cut into wedges
¾ cup chopped fresh parsley
3 tablespoons olive oil
2 tablespoons plus 1 cup chopped green onions

6 tablespoons (¾ stick) butter
2 tablespoons all purpose flour
1 8-ounce bottle clam juice
1 cup half and half
1 8-ounce package cream cheese
1½ cups (packed) grated Swiss cheese (about 6 ounces)
1 tablespoon prepared horseradish
2 teaspoons Worcestershire sauce
1 teaspoon cayenne pepper
1 pound crabmeat, drained

Preheat oven to 350°F. Place pita wedges on baking sheet. Mix ¼ cup parsley, oil and 2 tablespoons green onions in small bowl; brush over pita wedges. Bake until crisp, about 20 minutes. Cool. (*Can be prepared 1 day ahead. Store airtight at room temperature.*)

Melt butter in heavy large sauce-pan over medium heat. Add ¾ cup green onions; sauté 2 minutes. Add flour; whisk 1 minute. Gradually whisk in clam juice. Boil until mixture thickens, stirring often, about 3 minutes. Whisk in half and half and bring to boil. Boil 1 minute, stirring constantly. Reduce heat to low. Add both cheeses, horseradish, Worcestershire sauce and cayenne pepper; stir until cheeses melt. (*Can be made 1 day ahead. Cover and chill. Before continuing, rewarm over low heat, stirring constantly.*) Mix crab, remaining ½ cup parsley and remaining ¼ cup green onions into cheese and stir over medium-low heat to warm through.

Spoon crab dip into bowl. Set bowl in center of large platter. Surround with pita.

Spreads

GREEN OLIVE SPREAD
Try this on pita bread or baguette slices.

MAKES 2 CUPS

1 cup chopped pitted green olives (such as Sicilian)
½ cup chopped walnuts
½ cup chopped parsley
½ cup chopped green onions
½ cup chopped onion
⅓ cup olive oil
3 tablespoons fresh lemon juice
¼ teaspoon dried crushed red pepper

Combine all ingredients in processor. Using about 5 on/off turns, process just until mixture holds together (do not puree). Transfer to small bowl. Season to taste with salt and pepper. (*Can be prepared 1 day ahead. Cover and refrigerate.*)

CHIVE-GOAT CHEESE SPREAD

Making this at least a day ahead will allow the flavors to blend.

8 SERVINGS

8 ounces soft fresh goat cheese
  (such as Montrachet), room
  temperature
4 ounces cream cheese, room
  temperature
6 tablespoons minced fresh chives
  (about 1 ounce)
1 garlic clove, pressed
12 whole long fresh chives
1 French bread baguette, sliced

Combine goat cheese, cream cheese, minced chives and garlic in medium bowl. Stir with fork until well blended. Place large piece of plastic wrap on work surface. Arrange whole chives in crisscross pattern atop center of plastic. Spoon cheese into center of chives, forming 4- to 5-inch round. Lift edges of plastic, wrapping chives around cheese and covering cheese completely. Refrigerate overnight. *(Can be prepared 2 days ahead. Keep refrigerated.)* Remove plastic wrap from cheese. Place cheese on platter; surround with baguette slices and serve.

SMOKED SALMON SPREAD WITH PUMPERNICKEL BREAD

This easy-to-make spread looks impressive served in a hollowed-out loaf of bread. A dry champagne goes with it nicely.

6 SERVINGS

8 ounces smoked salmon
1 8-ounce package cream cheese,
  room temperature
3 green onions, chopped
¼ cup milk
2 tablespoons fresh lemon juice
2 teaspoons Worcestershire sauce
½ teaspoon hot pepper sauce
  (such as Tabasco)
¼ cup drained capers
2 tablespoons chopped fresh dill

1 ¾-pound round loaf pumpernickel
  or sourdough bread (unsliced)
  Fresh dill sprigs
  Cocktail-size pumpernickel bread
  slices, cut crosswise in half

Blend first 7 ingredients in processor until smooth. Transfer to bowl. Mix in capers and chopped dill. Cover and refrigerate until cold, about 2 hours. *(Can be prepared 1 day ahead.)*

Cut off top of loaf. Cut out center of bread, leaving 1½-inch bread shell on all sides (reserve cut-out bread for another use). Spoon salmon mixture into center of loaf. Place loaf on platter; prop bread lid decoratively at side. Garnish with dill sprigs. Arrange bread slices around loaf.

SMOKED FISH PÂTÉ WITH PITA CHIPS

6 SERVINGS

4 pita bread rounds, each cut into
   8 wedges
3 tablespoons olive oil
   Garlic salt

1 pound smoked fish (such as
   bluefish, trout or chub), skinned,
   boned, chopped
½ cup chopped green onion
¼ cup fresh lemon juice
¼ cup cream cheese, room
   temperature

Preheat oven to 350°F. Place pita wedges on baking sheet. Brush pita with olive oil. Season with garlic salt. Bake pita until crisp, about 7 minutes.

Mix fish, green onion, lemon juice and cream cheese in medium bowl to blend. Spoon pâté into bowl. (*Pita chips and pâté can be prepared 1 day ahead. Store chips in airtight container at room temperature. Cover and refrigerate pâté.*) Place pâté on platter. Surround with pita chips.

PRÊT-À-PÂTÉ

As a child, you may not have liked broccoli, cauliflower and carrots, but you'll love them in the vegetable pâté from Les Trois Petits Cochons. Rich and creamy, with a flaky puff pastry crust, it is a delicious warm or cold appetizer. Call 800-537-7283.

SMOKED TURKEY AND CHEESE SPREAD

Delicious on crackers or as a filling for small tea sandwiches.

MAKES ABOUT 2¼ CUPS

1 8-ounce package cream cheese,
   room temperature
3 tablespoons mayonnaise
1 cup coarsely chopped fully cooked
   smoked turkey (about 6 ounces)
½ cup plus 2 tablespoons chopped
   pecans
6 tablespoons chopped fresh parsley

Combine cream cheese and mayonnaise in processor; blend until smooth. Add turkey and process, using on/off turns, until coarse paste forms. Transfer mixture to medium bowl. Mix in ½ cup pecans and 4 tablespoons parsley. Season to taste with salt and pepper. Spoon into small serving bowl. Sprinkle top with remaining 2 tablespoons pecans and 2 tablespoons parsley. (*Can be prepared 3 days ahead. Cover and refrigerate. Let stand at room temperature 30 minutes before serving.*)

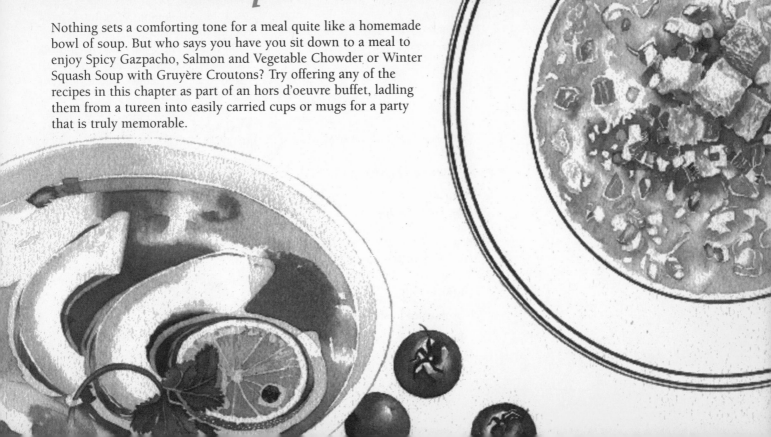

Soups

Nothing sets a comforting tone for a meal quite like a homemade bowl of soup. But who says you have you sit down to a meal to enjoy Spicy Gazpacho, Salmon and Vegetable Chowder or Winter Squash Soup with Gruyère Croutons? Try offering any of the recipes in this chapter as part of an hors d'oeuvre buffet, ladling them from a tureen into easily carried cups or mugs for a party that is truly memorable.

Cold Soups

SPICY GAZPACHO

8 SERVINGS

4 large tomatoes
3 cups hot and spicy vegetable juice
2 cups chopped seeded peeled cucumber
1⅔ cups chopped green bell pepper
1 cup chopped onion
¼ cup olive oil
¼ cup red wine vinegar
2 tablespoons fresh lemon juice
2 tablespoons Worcestershire sauce

Chopped fresh parsley

Bring large pot of water to boil. Add tomatoes; blanch 15 seconds. Drain and cool. Peel, seed and coarsely chop tomatoes. Transfer to large bowl. Add all remaining ingredients except parsley. Working in batches, blend mixture to coarse puree in blender. Season with salt and pepper. Cover and chill until cold, about 3 hours. (*Can be made 1 day ahead; keep chilled.*)

Ladle soup into bowls. Sprinkle with parsley and serve.

CHILLED ZUCCHINI-CUMIN SOUP

4 SERVINGS

1 teaspoon olive oil
1 large onion, chopped
1½ teaspoons ground cumin
1½ pounds zucchini, trimmed, cut into ¾-inch pieces
2 14½-ounce cans low-salt chicken broth

⅓ cup chopped fresh basil

4 tablespoons plain nonfat yogurt
Sliced fresh basil

Heat oil in heavy medium saucepan over medium heat. Add onion; sauté until tender, about 5 minutes. Add cumin; stir until aromatic, about 30 seconds. Mix in zucchini. Add broth; bring soup to boil. Reduce heat; simmer until zucchini is very tender, about 30 minutes. Cool slightly.

Mix ⅓ cup chopped basil into soup. Working in batches, puree soup in blender until smooth. Transfer to bowl. Season with salt and pepper. Cover; chill until cold, about 3 hours. (*Can be made 1 day ahead. Keep refrigerated.*)

Ladle soup into bowls. Top each with 1 tablespoon yogurt and sliced basil.

COLD TOMATO-THYME SOUP WITH GRILLED GARLIC CROUTONS

Tomato time is the best time to put this do-ahead soup on the menu.

6 SERVINGS

5 tablespoons olive oil
  (preferably extra-virgin)
2 cups finely chopped onions
¾ cup finely chopped peeled carrots
2½ teaspoons finely chopped garlic
1 bay leaf
3 pounds ripe tomatoes, halved,
  seeded, chopped (about 5 cups)
3 cups canned low-salt chicken broth
3 tablespoons finely chopped fresh
  thyme or 1 tablespoon dried

1 cup hickory smoke chips, soaked
  in water 30 minutes, drained
3 ¾-inch-thick slices sourdough
  bread
1 garlic clove, halved

Fresh thyme sprigs (optional)

Heat 4 tablespoons oil in heavy large pot over medium heat. Add onions, carrots, finely chopped garlic and bay leaf. Cover; cook until carrots are tender, stirring occasionally, about 10 minutes. Add tomatoes. Cover; cook until tomatoes release juices, about 10 minutes. Uncover; cook until juices evaporate, stirring often, about 20 minutes. Add broth and chopped thyme. Partially cover pot and simmer until mixture is reduced to 6 cups, stirring occasionally, about 10 minutes longer.

Cool soup slightly. Discard bay leaf. Puree half of soup in blender. Stir into soup in pot. Season with salt and pepper. Chill uncovered until cold, then cover. *(Can be made 1 day ahead. Keep chilled.)*

Prepare barbecue (medium heat). Place smoke chips in 8x6-inch foil packet with open top. Set packet atop coals about 5 minutes before grilling. Brush 1 tablespoon oil over both sides of bread slices. Grill bread until lightly browned, about 2 minutes per side. Rub garlic clove halves over bread. Cut bread into ¾-inch cubes.

Divide cold soup among bowls. Top with croutons. Garnish with thyme.

Hot Soups

TOMATO, DILL AND WHITE CHEDDAR SOUP

If you're serving people who don't like spicy foods, eliminate the cayenne pepper.

6 SERVINGS

2 tablespoons olive oil
3 cups chopped leeks (white and pale green parts only)
4 28-ounce cans diced tomatoes with juices
4½ cups canned low-salt chicken broth
6 tablespoons (packed) chopped fresh dill or 2 tablespoons dried dillweed
¼ teaspoon cayenne pepper

½ cup light sour cream

4 ounces chilled sharp white cheddar cheese, sliced
Fresh dill sprigs

Heat oil in heavy large pot over medium heat. Add leeks and sauté until tender, about 6 minutes. Add tomatoes and their juices, broth, chopped dill and cayenne and bring to boil. Reduce heat and simmer uncovered until tomatoes are very soft and flavors blend, about 20 minutes.

Working in batches, puree soup in processor until smooth. Return to same pot. *(Can be made 1 day ahead. Cover and chill.)* Bring to simmer over medium-low heat. Season with salt and pepper. Gradually whisk in sour cream (do not boil).

Ladle soup into bowls. Arrange cheese atop each. Garnish with dill sprigs.

SPICED CARROT SOUP WITH CILANTRO YOGURT

4 TO 6 SERVINGS

1 cup plain low-fat yogurt
¼ cup chopped fresh cilantro

1 tablespoon butter
1½ cups chopped onions
1 pound large carrots (about 4), peeled, coarsely chopped
1 large russet potato, peeled, chopped
1 teaspoon ground cumin
½ teaspoon ground ginger
½ teaspoon ground cinnamon
Pinch of dried crushed red pepper
2 cups canned chicken broth
2 cups water

Combine yogurt and cilantro in blender and puree. Transfer to small bowl.

Melt butter in heavy large saucepan over medium heat. Add onions; sauté until soft, about 6 minutes. Add carrots, potato and spices; stir 1 minute. Add broth and water; bring to boil. Reduce heat to medium-low, cover and simmer until vegetables are tender, about 20 minutes.

Puree soup in batches in blender. Return to pan; season with salt and pepper. Rewarm soup; ladle into bowls. Garnish with swirl of cilantro yogurt.

WHITE BEAN, ESCAROLE AND BELL PEPPER SOUP

A delicious and colorful starter.

6 SERVINGS

2 tablespoons olive oil
1 large onion, chopped
1 yellow bell pepper, coarsely chopped
1 red bell pepper, coarsely chopped
½ medium head escarole, sliced
⅛ teaspoon dried crushed red pepper
4½ cups canned low-salt chicken broth
1 15-ounce can cannellini (white kidney beans), rinsed, drained

1½ teaspoons dried marjoram
Grated Pecorino Romano cheese

Heat oil in heavy large pot over medium-high heat. Add onion and bell peppers; sauté until beginning to brown, about 15 minutes. Add escarole and crushed red pepper; sauté until escarole wilts, about 3 minutes. Add broth, beans and marjoram. Simmer 10 minutes. Season with salt and pepper. Sprinkle with cheese.

REDUCED-FAT POTATO CHOWDER

The fat may be reduced here, but the flavor isn't: Even hearty appetites will be satisfied with this rib-sticking winter soup.

MAKES ABOUT 6 CUPS

8 bacon slices, coarsely chopped
1 cup chopped onion
1 cup chopped celery
1 cup sliced carrots

1 pound red-skinned potatoes, scrubbed, diced
2 cups canned low-salt chicken broth
¼ teaspoon garlic powder
1½ cups nonfat milk
1 10½-ounce can condensed reduced-fat cream of celery soup
¼ cup chopped parsley

Cook bacon in heavy large pot over medium heat until brown and crisp. Using slotted spoon, transfer bacon to paper towels and drain. Pour off all but 1 tablespoon drippings from pot. Add onion, celery and carrots to pot. Sauté until soft, about 10 minutes. Add potatoes, chicken broth and garlic powder. Cover pot and simmer soup until vegetables are tender, stirring occasionally, about 15 minutes. Add milk and condensed soup and simmer 5 minutes. Season soup to taste with salt and pepper. Stir in parsley. Ladle soup into bowls; top with bacon and serve.

Winter Squash Soup with Gruyère Croutons

In France, this soup would be prepared with a baking pumpkin. A mixture of butternut and acorn squashes mimics the French pumpkin's exceptional taste and texture.

8 SERVINGS

SOUP

¼ cup (½ stick) butter
1 large onion, finely chopped
4 large garlic cloves, chopped
3 14½-ounce cans low-salt chicken broth
4 cups 1-inch pieces peeled butternut squash (about 1½ pounds)
4 cups 1-inch pieces peeled acorn squash (about 1½ pounds)
1¼ teaspoons minced fresh thyme
1¼ teaspoons minced fresh sage

¼ cup whipping cream
2 teaspoons sugar

CROUTONS

2 tablespoons (¼ stick) butter
24 ½-inch-thick baguette bread slices
1 cup grated Gruyère cheese
1 teaspoon minced fresh thyme
1 teaspoon minced fresh sage

FOR SOUP: Melt butter in large pot over medium heat. Add onion and garlic and sauté until tender, about 10 minutes. Add broth, all squash and herbs; bring to boil. Reduce heat, cover and simmer until squash is very tender, about 20 minutes.

Working in batches, puree soup in blender. Return soup to same pot. Stir in cream and sugar; bring to simmer. Season with salt and pepper. *(Can be made 1 day ahead. Chill. Rewarm over medium heat before serving.)*

FOR CROUTONS: Preheat broiler. Butter 1 side of each bread slice. Arrange bread, buttered side up, on baking sheet. Broil until golden, about 1 minute. Turn over. Sprinkle cheese, then thyme and sage over. Sprinkle with salt and pepper. Broil until cheese melts, about 1 minute.

Ladle soup into bowls. Top each with croutons and serve.

Salmon and Vegetable Chowder

4 TO 6 SERVINGS

1 tablespoon vegetable oil
1 leek (white and pale green parts only), sliced
1 teaspoon fennel seeds
1 large russet potato, peeled, diced
1 large zucchini, diced
1 cup frozen corn kernels
1 carrot, diced
2 tablespoons chopped fresh thyme or 2 teaspoons dried
3 cups canned low-salt chicken broth
½ cup dry white wine
1 pound skinless salmon fillet, cut into ¾-inch pieces
1 cup whipping cream

Heat oil in heavy large pot over medium heat. Add leek and fennel seeds and sauté until leek is tender but not brown, about 5 minutes. Add potato, zucchini, corn, carrot and half of thyme. Stir 2 minutes. Add chicken broth and wine; simmer until potato is tender, about 15 minutes. Add salmon and cream. Simmer until salmon is just opaque in center, about 5 minutes. Season chowder to taste with salt and pepper.

Ladle chowder into deep bowls. Sprinkle chowder with remaining thyme and serve immediately.

CREAMY CARROT SOUP

6 TO 8 SERVINGS

5 large carrots (about 1½ pounds), peeled, cut into ½-inch pieces
3½ cups canned low-salt chicken broth
1 large onion, peeled, quartered
1¼ teaspoons chopped fresh thyme or ½ teaspoon dried
1 large bay leaf
¼ teaspoon (scant) ground allspice

¾ cup drained canned small white beans
1 cup milk

Combine carrots, broth, onion, thyme, bay leaf and allspice in large pot and bring to boil. Reduce heat, cover and simmer until carrots are tender, about 15 minutes. Remove bay leaf.

Working in batches, puree soup in blender until smooth, adding some of beans with each batch. Return soup to same pot; add milk. Stir over low heat until heated through. Season with salt and pepper and serve.

ALL SOUPED UP

Some of the East Coast's best shellfish inspired the delicious soups from Denzer's. Their Maryland crab soup, "Carolina conch" chowder and queen conch chowder are all rich and robust, with homemade taste. Call 800-224-2811.

CHICKEN, CORN AND NOODLE SOUP WITH SAFFRON

8 SERVINGS

9 cups canned low-salt chicken broth
1 3-pound cut-up chicken; neck, gizzard and heart reserved

3 tablespoons butter
2 cups chopped onions
1 cup diced peeled carrots
¾ cup diced celery
2 large garlic cloves, minced
¼ teaspoon dried thyme
¼ teaspoon crumbled saffron threads
2 ounces dried wide egg noodles
1 cup frozen corn kernels
2 tablespoons minced fresh parsley
2 tablespoons minced celery leaves

Combine broth, chicken pieces, neck, gizzard and heart in large pot. Bring to boil. Reduce heat; cover partially and simmer until chicken is cooked through, about 20 minutes. Using tongs, remove chicken pieces and giblets from broth. Cool slightly. Remove skin from breasts and leg-thigh pieces. Cut enough chicken meat to measure 1 cup. Reserve remaining cooked chicken for another use. Strain broth into large bowl. Chill broth until fat solidifies on surface, about 6 hours. (*Broth can be made 2 days ahead. Keep chilled.*) Scrape fat from surface of broth and discard.

Melt butter in heavy large pot over medium-low heat. Add onions, carrots, celery, garlic and thyme. Cover; cook until vegetables soften, stirring occasionally, about 10 minutes. Add broth and bring to boil. Reduce heat; simmer until vegetables are almost tender, about 15 minutes. Add saffron. (*Can be made 1 day ahead. Cover; chill. Bring to boil before continuing.*) Add noodles; simmer 5 minutes. Add 1 cup chicken and corn; simmer until noodles are tender, about 5 minutes. Add parsley and celery leaves. Season with salt and pepper.

YUKON GOLD POTATO AND CHIVE SOUP

This soup has the classic flavors of a baked potato topped with sour cream and chives. It would be perfect as a starter to a meal of steak and salad, or terrific teamed with crusty bread for lunch.

6 SERVINGS

7 cups (or more) canned low-salt chicken broth
2½ pounds Yukon Gold potatoes, peeled, sliced (about 7 cups)
3 large garlic cloves, peeled

⅔ cup half and half
½ cup minced fresh chives

Sour cream

Combine 7 cups chicken broth, potatoes and garlic cloves in large pot. Bring to boil. Reduce heat to medium; cover and simmer until potatoes are very tender, about 25 minutes.

Working in batches, puree soup in

blender until smooth. Return to same pot. Add half and half and bring to simmer. Thin with more broth if soup is too thick. Season to taste with salt and pepper. Stir in chives. *(Can be prepared 1 day ahead. Cover and refrigerate. Rewarm over low heat, stirring frequently.)*

Ladle soup into bowls. Top with dollop of sour cream and serve.

ALL THOSE CHIVES

The word *chives* has a history of its own, stemming from the same root as *civet*, a kind of stew flavored with chives or other members of the onion family. In old cookbooks, chives are often referred to as *cives*, a derivation of the Latin word for onions. In the Middle Ages, they were sometimes known as rush-leeks; the Greek words for "rush" (*schoinos*) and "leek" (*prason*) are the source of the botanical name, *Allium schoenoprasum*. (*Allium* is the genus that includes the onion family.) Rush garlic is also what early settlers along Lakes Superior and Huron called the wild chives they found growing there.

Today, in addition to wild chives, there are several other varieties of this popular herb with the long, hollow leaves and lovely purple flowers. Among them are pink and white chives, denoting the colors of the plants' flowers, as well as garlic chives, which are sometimes called Chinese chives and have a more pronounced garlicky taste.

One thing all chives have in common is that they don't take well to drying, losing most of their flavor in the process. You can freeze them, but these days fresh chives are available year-round in most markets. Better yet, snip them fresh off the plant. This can be done more easily than you might imagine, even in the last dreary days of winter, since chives grow well in a pot on the kitchen windowsill. Let the plant reach six inches in height before you begin to snip; then, when you do, leave an inch or two of leaf to keep the bulbs going.

Mexican Lime Soup

A homey yet sophisticated soup that's great for casual entertaining.

6 SERVINGS

2 tablespoons olive oil
6 garlic cloves, sliced
6 small skinless boneless chicken breast halves, cut crosswise into ½-inch-wide strips
1½ teaspoons dried oregano
9 cups canned low-salt chicken broth
⅓ cup fresh lime juice

1½ cups coarsely crushed tortilla chips
2 avocados, peeled, pitted, diced
3 tomatoes, chopped
3 green onions, sliced
Chopped fresh cilantro
Minced jalapeño chilies
Lime slices

Heat oil in heavy large pot over medium heat. Add garlic and stir 20 seconds. Add chicken and oregano to pot; sprinkle with salt and pepper. Sauté 3 minutes. Add broth and lime juice and bring to simmer. Reduce heat to medium-low and simmer gently until chicken is cooked through, about 8 minutes. Season soup to taste with salt and pepper.

Divide crushed tortilla chips among 6 bowls. Ladle soup into bowls. Top soup with avocados, tomatoes, green onions, cilantro and jalapeños. Garnish with lime slices and serve.

Fennel, Leek and Spinach Soup

Ideal for any spring occasion.

8 SERVINGS

6 tablespoons (¾ stick) unsalted margarine
6 cups chopped fresh fennel bulbs
4 cups chopped leeks (white and pale green parts only)
6 cups chicken broth
⅔ cup (packed) fresh spinach leaves

Melt margarine in large pot over medium heat. Add fennel and leeks. Sauté until just translucent, about 15 minutes. Add broth and cover pot. Simmer until vegetables are tender, about 20 minutes.

Puree soup in small batches in blender until smooth, adding spinach to last batch before pureeing. Return soup to same pot. Season with salt and pepper. *(Can be prepared 1 day ahead. Refrigerate until cold, then cover and keep refrigerated.)*

Rewarm soup over low heat, stirring occasionally. Ladle into bowls and serve.

POTATO SOUP WITH BLUE CHEESE AND BACON

6 TO 8 SERVINGS

8 bacon slices

2 cups chopped onion
1 large leek (white and pale green parts only), chopped
3 celery stalks, chopped
2 medium carrots, peeled, chopped
3¾ cups canned low-salt chicken broth
1 large potato (about 10 ounces), peeled, chopped
1 cup dry white wine

4 ounces blue cheese, crumbled

Cook bacon in heavy large pot over medium heat until brown and crisp. Using tongs, transfer bacon to paper towels and drain. Crumble bacon.

Spoon off all but 2 tablespoons bacon drippings from pot. Add onion, leek, celery and carrots to pot. Cover, reduce heat to low and cook until vegetables begin to soften and color, about 15 minutes. Add broth, potato and wine. Bring to boil. Partially cover pot. Simmer until all vegetables are tender, about 30 minutes. Remove from heat.

Place cheese in processor. Add 1½ cups hot soup. Blend until cheese melts and mixture is smooth. Return cheese mixture to soup in pot and stir to blend. Season soup to taste with salt and pepper. (*Can be prepared 1 day ahead. Cover soup and wrap bacon; refrigerate.*)

Stir soup over low heat until heated through. Ladle soup into bowls. Sprinkle bacon over and serve.

LEMON CHICKEN SOUP WITH FRESH SPINACH AND FARFALLE

4 TO 6 SERVINGS

2 tablespoons olive oil
1 large onion, chopped
2 large garlic cloves, finely chopped
3 celery stalks, chopped
2 carrots, diced
1 large red bell pepper, chopped
8 cups (or more) canned low-salt chicken broth
2 cups dried farfalle (bow-tie) pasta

2 cups diced cooked chicken
2 tablespoons fresh lemon juice
2 teaspoons grated lemon peel
½ 10-ounce package ready-to-use spinach leaves (about 6 cups)

Grated Parmesan cheese

Heat oil in heavy large pot over medium heat. Add onion and garlic and stir 1 minute. Add celery, carrots and red bell pepper and sauté until vegetables are tender, about 8 minutes. Add 8 cups broth and bring soup to boil. Reduce heat to medium-low; simmer to blend flavors, about 20 minutes. Add pasta and simmer until pasta is tender, stirring occasionally, about 10 minutes.

Mix chicken, lemon juice and lemon peel into soup. Add spinach. Simmer until spinach wilts but is still bright green, stirring occasionally, about 3 minutes. Thin soup with additional chicken broth, if desired. Season soup to taste with salt and pepper.

Ladle soup into bowls. Serve, passing cheese separately.

POTATO, LEEK AND ONION SOUP WITH GARLIC CHEESE TOASTS

6 TO 8 SERVINGS

5 tablespoons olive oil
3 large leeks (white and pale green parts only), sliced
1½ pounds russet potatoes, peeled, diced
1 large white onion, chopped
4 14½-ounce cans vegetable broth

3 large garlic cloves, chopped
1½ cups grated Swiss cheese
8 slices sourdough bread

½ cup chopped fresh chives or green onion tops

Heat 4 tablespoons oil in heavy large pot over medium-low heat. Add leeks, potatoes and onion. Sauté until onion is tender, stirring occasionally, about 12 minutes. Add broth and bring soup to boil. Reduce heat to medium-low. Simmer until all vegetables are tender, about 20 minutes. Working in batches, puree 5 cups soup in blender. Return puree to soup in pot. Season with salt and pepper. (*Can be made 1 day ahead. Refrigerate uncovered until cold. Cover and keep refrigerated.*)

Preheat oven to 350°F. Stir remaining 1 tablespoon oil and garlic in small skillet over low heat until garlic is fragrant, about 1 minute; remove from heat and cool. Add cheese to garlic in skillet; toss to combine. Arrange bread slices on baking sheet. Spoon cheese mixture onto bread slices, dividing equally. Bake toasts until cheese melts, about 10 minutes.

Bring soup to simmer over medium heat, stirring frequently. Ladle into bowls. Sprinkle generously with chives. Serve, passing toasts separately.

Salads

Some salads, such as Mixed Greens with Goat Cheese Crostini or Arugula with Prosciutto and Mango, are meant to be individually plated and presented as starters. Others, however, hold greater potential to be served and eaten as part of a buffet. Try Jicama and Grilled Red Pepper Slaw, Layered Rice Salad with Red and Green Salsas or Smorgasbord Salad with Smoked Salmon and Dill Sauce the next time you entertain a crowd.

Vegetable Salads

CURLY ENDIVE WITH TOASTED ALMOND DRESSING

6 SERVINGS

3 tablespoons minced shallots
2 tablespoons red wine vinegar
5 tablespoons extra-virgin olive oil
¼ cup whole almonds, toasted, finely chopped

8 cups bite-size pieces curly endive

Whisk shallots and red wine vinegar in medium bowl. Gradually whisk in olive oil. Whisk in almonds. Season dressing to taste with salt and pepper.

Toss curly endive in large bowl with enough dressing to coat.

MIXED GREENS AND WALNUTS WITH BUTTERMILK DRESSING

6 SERVINGS

1 tablespoon fresh lime juice
1 tablespoon balsamic vinegar
½ teaspoon Dijon mustard
⅓ cup low-fat buttermilk
1 tablespoon walnut oil or olive oil

8 ounces mixed baby greens
¼ cup walnut pieces, toasted
3 tablespoons chopped fresh parsley

Whisk lime juice, vinegar and mustard in medium bowl to blend. Gradually whisk in buttermilk, then oil. Season to taste with salt and pepper. (*Can be prepared 6 hours ahead. Cover and refrigerate.*)

Combine mixed greens, walnuts and parsley in large bowl. Toss with enough dressing to coat. Season to taste with salt and pepper and serve.

CORN, TOMATO AND BASIL SALAD

Fresh colorful and simple, this salad is the essence of summer.

6 SERVINGS

6 large ears white corn, husked
5 tablespoons olive oil
1 tablespoon finely chopped garlic
½ cup (packed) thinly sliced fresh basil

5 plum tomatoes, seeded, chopped
3 tablespoons balsamic vinegar

Using large knife, cut corn kernels from cob. Heat 2 tablespoons oil in heavy large skillet over medium-high heat. Add garlic; sauté 1 minute. Add corn; sauté until just cooked through, about 5 minutes. Remove from heat. Add half of basil.

Transfer corn mixture to large bowl. Cool slightly, stirring occasionally. Stir in tomatoes, vinegar, 3 tablespoons oil and remaining basil. Season with salt and pepper. Cover; chill 3 hours or up to 8 hours.

MIXED GREENS WITH GOAT CHEESE CROSTINI

The warm goat cheese toasts make delicious croutons for the salad, but they would also be an easy hors d'oeuvre in their own right.

2 SERVINGS

8 ½-inch-thick diagonally cut
    baguette slices (about 4 inches
    long by 1½ inches wide)
8 tablespoons (4 ounces) soft fresh
    goat cheese (such as Montrachet)

¼ cup olive oil
2 tablespoons red wine vinegar
1 small garlic clove, minced
5 cups mixed baby greens
2 tablespoons chopped drained
    oil-packed sun-dried tomatoes
2 tablespoons pine nuts, toasted

Preheat broiler. Spread each baguette slice with 1 tablespoon goat cheese. Arrange on baking sheet, cheese side up.

Whisk oil, vinegar and garlic in large bowl to blend. Add greens, sun-dried tomatoes and pine nuts; toss to combine. Season salad to taste with salt and pepper. Divide salad between 2 plates.

Broil crostini just until goat cheese softens and begins to melt, about 1 minute. Arrange 4 crostini atop each salad and serve.

HARVEST ROOT VEGETABLE SALAD

Honey, shallots and some raspberry vinegar brighten up the flavor of a colorful salad.

6 SERVINGS

3 large beets (about 12 ounces total)

1 large rutabaga (about 10 ounces),
    peeled, cut into matchstick-size
    strips
1 large carrot, peeled, cut into
    matchstick-size strips
1 large parsnip, peeled, cut into
    matchstick-size strips
1 turnip, peeled, cut into
    matchstick-size strips

¾ cup vegetable oil
¼ cup walnut oil or olive oil
¼ cup fresh lemon juice
2 tablespoons raspberry vinegar or
    red wine vinegar
1 tablespoon honey
2 shallots, minced

½ cup chopped fresh chives or
    green onions
1 bunch spinach, trimmed
¼ cup chopped toasted walnuts
    (optional)

Preheat oven to 400°F. Wrap beets in foil. Bake until tender, about 1 hour. Cool; peel beets. Cut into matchstick-size strips.

Bring large pot of water to boil. Add rutabaga, carrot, parsnip and turnip strips and boil until crisp-tender, about 3 minutes. Drain. Transfer to bowl of ice water and cool. Drain well. (*Can be prepared 1 day ahead. Cover and refrigerate beets and blanched vegetables separately.)*

Whisk both oils, lemon juice, vinegar and honey in small bowl to blend. Mix in shallots. Season with salt and pepper. *(Dressing can be made 6 hours ahead. Cover and let stand at room temperature.)*

Combine beets and blanched vegetables in large bowl. Add chives and enough dressing to coat. Season salad with salt and pepper. Arrange spinach around edge of platter. Mound salad in center. Sprinkle with nuts, if desired, and serve.

EGGPLANT, TOMATO AND BELL PEPPER SALAD

This light-tasting and refreshing salad is great piled into pita bread with yogurt, spooned onto lettuce leaves as a first course or served with crackers as an appetizer.

MAKES 4 CUPS

1   1½-pound eggplant
    Coarse salt

1   cup diced seeded plum tomatoes
½   cup diced green bell pepper
½   cup diced red bell pepper
½   cup chopped onion
⅓   cup olive oil
3   tablespoons chopped fresh parsley
2   tablespoons fresh lemon juice
2   large garlic cloves, minced
    Brine-cured olives (optional)

Preheat oven to 400°F. Line baking sheet with foil. Pierce eggplant several times with fork. Place eggplant on prepared sheet and bake until cooked through and soft to touch, turning once, about 40 minutes. Cool briefly; peel. Cut eggplant into ½-inch cubes. Place in colander, sprinkle lightly with coarse salt and let drain 15 minutes.

Place eggplant in large bowl. Add tomatoes, green and red bell peppers, onion, olive oil, parsley, lemon juice and garlic. Toss to blend well. Season to taste with salt and pepper. Cover and refrigerate at least 2 hours before serving. *(Can be prepared 1 day ahead. Keep refrigerated.)* Garnish with olives, if desired.

Green Bean Caesar Salad

This reduced-fat version hits all the flavor notes of the original Caesar.

8 SERVINGS

1 cup plain nonfat yogurt
1 cup fat-free bottled Italian dressing
4 garlic cloves, chopped
2 tablespoons Dijon mustard
2 teaspoons Worcestershire sauce

1 pound green beans, trimmed, halved
2 heads romaine lettuce, torn into bite-size pieces
2 small heads radicchio, thinly sliced
8 tablespoons grated Parmesan cheese

Combine first 5 ingredients in small bowl; whisk to blend. Season with pepper.

Cook beans in medium pot of boiling salted water until crisp-tender, about 4 minutes. Drain. Rinse with cold water; drain again. Combine beans, romaine, radicchio and 4 tablespoons cheese in large bowl. Add dressing and toss to coat. Sprinkle with 4 tablespoons cheese.

Jicama and Grilled Red Pepper Slaw

Sweet and crunchy jicama and smoky grill-roasted peppers and green onions combine in this attractive salad.

6 SERVINGS

1 cup hickory smoke chips, soaked in water 30 minutes, drained
8 large green onions, trimmed
4½ tablespoons corn oil
3 large red bell peppers

5 tablespoons fresh orange juice
1½ tablespoons fresh lime juice
1 tablespoon honey
¾ teaspoon ground cumin
1 jicama (about 18 ounces), peeled, cut into matchstick-size strips

Prepare barbecue (medium-high heat). Place smoke chips in 8x6-inch foil packet with open top. Set packet atop coals about 5 minutes before grilling. Brush green onions with 1½ tablespoons oil. Grill until lightly browned, turning often, about 4 minutes. Cut onions into ¼-inch pieces. Place in large bowl. Grill peppers until lightly charred, turning often, about 10 minutes. Enclose in paper bag; let stand 10 minutes. Peel and seed peppers; cut into ¼-inch-wide strips. Add to onions.

Whisk orange juice, lime juice, honey, cumin and 3 tablespoons oil in small bowl. (*Vegetables and dressing can be made 8 hours ahead. Cover separately and refrigerate.*) Add jicama and dressing to grilled vegetables; toss to coat. Season with salt and pepper.

Eggplant and Watercress Salad with Sesame

4 SERVINGS

1 cup hickory smoke chips, soaked
 in water 30 minutes, drained
1 large eggplant (about 1½ pounds),
 sliced into ¾-inch-thick rounds
4 tablespoons corn oil

1 tablespoon sesame seeds

2 tablespoons seasoned rice vinegar*
1½ teaspoons soy sauce
¾ teaspoon Oriental sesame oil
⅛ teaspoon dried crushed red pepper
1 bunch watercress, trimmed

Prepare barbecue (medium heat). Place smoke chips in 8x6-inch foil packet with open top. Set packet atop coals about 5 minutes before grilling. Brush eggplant with 2 tablespoons corn oil. Grill until cooked, about 5 minutes per side. Cut into ¾-inch cubes. Place in large bowl.

Toast sesame seeds in heavy small skillet over medium-low heat until light brown, about 5 minutes.

Whisk vinegar, soy sauce, sesame oil, crushed red pepper and 2 tablespoons corn oil in medium bowl. Add watercress to eggplant in large bowl. Toss with enough dressing to coat. Season with salt and pepper. Sprinkle sesame seeds over salad.

Also known as sushi vinegar; available at Asian markets and in the Asian section of some supermarkets.

Layered Nacho Salad

Make the salad in a clear glass bowl to show off the colors. Pass some purchased red wine vinaigrette or buttermilk dressing alongside.

8 TO 10 SERVINGS

2 large ripe avocados, peeled, pitted
2 cups (or more) purchased thick
 salsa (mild or medium-hot)
1 head red leaf lettuce, torn into
 bite-size pieces
3 cups shredded cooked chicken
3 cups broken tortilla chips
1 15-ounce can black beans, rinsed,
 drained
4 green onions, chopped
1 small green bell pepper, chopped
1 cup (packed) grated sharp
 cheddar cheese

Place avocados in medium bowl. Add ⅓ cup salsa and mash to chunky guacamole consistency. Season with salt and pepper.

Layer half of lettuce, chicken, chips, beans, green onions, bell pepper and cheese in large bowl. Top with half of guacamole and half of remaining salsa. Repeat layering with remaining ingredients. Use additional salsa to cover top if necessary. (*Can be made 3 hours ahead. Cover; chill.*)

Potato Salad with Sugar Snap Peas and Mustard Seed Dressing

A simple salad with a tangy dressing.

4 SERVINGS

⅓ cup olive oil
5 tablespoons whole grain Dijon
  mustard
3 tablespoons yellow mustard seeds
3 tablespoons (packed) chopped
  fresh dill
2 tablespoons white wine vinegar

1½ pounds medium-size red-skinned
  potatoes, each cut into 6 wedges,
  each wedge cut crosswise in half
8 ounces sugar snap peas, stringed
½ cup chopped red onion

Whisk first 5 ingredients in small bowl to blend. Season with salt and pepper.

Steam potatoes just until tender, about 10 minutes. Transfer to large bowl; add 3 tablespoons dressing and toss to coat. Steam sugar snap peas until just crisp-tender, about 2 minutes. Cool. Add to bowl with potatoes. Add red onion. Pour remaining dressing over salad; toss to coat. Season to taste with salt and pepper.

Roasted Beet Salad with Beet Greens and Feta

Good cooks never discard the nutritious beet greens. Here, the greens are combined with roasted beets, capers and feta in a Greek-inspired salad.

6 SERVINGS

6 tablespoons extra-virgin olive oil
2½ tablespoons red wine vinegar
1 tablespoon minced garlic

7 medium-large beets (about 3
  inches in diameter) with greens
1 cup water
2 tablespoons chopped drained
  capers
¾ cup crumbled feta cheese
  (about 3 ounces)

Preheat oven to 375°F. Whisk oil, vinegar and garlic in small bowl to blend. Season dressing generously with salt and pepper.

Cut green tops off beets; reserve tops. Arrange beets in single layer in 13x9x2-inch baking dish; add 1 cup water. Cover; bake until beets are tender when pierced with knife, about 1 hour 10 minutes. Peel beets while warm. Cut beets in half and slice thinly. Transfer to large bowl. Mix in capers and ¼ cup dressing. Season with salt and pepper.

Cut stems off beet greens; discard stems. Wash greens. Transfer greens, with some water still clinging to leaves, to large pot. Stir over high heat until just wilted but still bright green, about 4 minutes. Drain greens; squeeze out excess moisture. Cool; chop coarsely.

Transfer greens to medium bowl. Toss with enough dressing to coat. Season to taste with salt and pepper.

Arrange beets in center of platter. Surround with greens; sprinkle with feta. Drizzle with any remaining dressing.

Fruit Salads

SWEET ORANGE, MINT AND OLIVE SALAD

Serve this flavorful Moroccan-style salad as part of a colorful buffet.

6 SERVINGS

½ teaspoon coriander seeds
½ teaspoon cumin seeds
⅓ cup brine-cured black olives
   (such as Kalamata), pitted
¼ cup fresh orange juice
¼ cup chopped fresh mint
3 green onions, chopped

¼ teaspoon sugar

5 medium navel oranges, peel and
   white pith removed

Romaine lettuce leaves

Toast coriander seeds and cumin seeds in medium skillet over medium heat just until fragrant, about 2 minutes. Transfer spices to a heavy small plastic bag. Using flat side of knife, press on spices to crush coarsely. Transfer spices to large bowl. Add olives, orange juice, mint, green onions and sugar; stir to blend.

Cut oranges into ⅓-inch-thick rounds. Add orange rounds to olive mixture and stir gently to coat. Season to taste with salt and pepper. (*Can be prepared 1 hour ahead. Cover and refrigerate.*)

Arrange lettuce leaves on platter. Arrange orange mixture decoratively atop lettuce and serve.

Waldorf Salad with Lentils and Pine Nuts

An appealing update of the classic salad.

6 SERVINGS

¾ cup lentils

2 medium Granny Smith apples,
   halved, cored, diced
1 cup diced celery
½ cup regular or low-fat mayonnaise
3 tablespoons fresh lemon juice
½ teaspoon sugar
¼ teaspoon ground allspice
⅓ cup pine nuts, toasted

Cook lentils in medium saucepan of boiling salted water until just tender, about 25 minutes. Drain; rinse. Drain again.

Place lentils in large bowl. Add apples and celery. Whisk mayonnaise, lemon juice, sugar and allspice in small bowl to blend. Mix dressing into lentil salad. Season to taste with salt and pepper. Sprinkle with pine nuts. Cover and refrigerate at least 2 and up to 8 hours.

Roasted Fennel and Pear Salad with Balsamic-Pear Dressing

Roasting tones down the sharpness of the fennel and enhances the sweetness of the pears in this salad. The pears also combine with balsamic vinegar to make a delicious dressing without much added fat.

4 SERVINGS

2 firm but ripe pears, halved, cored
1 medium fennel bulb (about 8
   ounces), cored, quartered
1 teaspoon olive oil
⅓ cup canned low-salt chicken broth

2 tablespoons balsamic vinegar

6 cups (packed) mixed baby greens

Preheat oven to 400°F. Arrange pears, cut side up, in 8x8x2-inch glass baking dish; add fennel. Drizzle olive oil and chicken broth over pears and fennel. Roast 10 minutes. Turn pears and fennel over and roast until pears are just tender, about 5 minutes longer. Using slotted spoon, transfer pears to plate. Continue roasting fennel until tender, about 15 minutes longer. Transfer fennel to plate with pears, reserving any cooking liquid. Thinly slice fennel and 2 pear halves lengthwise. Cool completely.

Peel remaining 2 pear halves. Transfer peeled pears to processor. Add reserved cooking liquid and vinegar to processor and blend until very smooth. Season dressing with salt and pepper.

Divide greens among 4 plates. Top with fennel and pear slices. Drizzle some dressing over each salad. Serve, passing remaining dressing separately.

Spinach and Apple Salad with Crispy Almonds

6 TO 8 SERVINGS

¼ cup minced onion
3 tablespoons apple cider vinegar
3 tablespoons white wine vinegar
2 tablespoons sesame seeds
¼ teaspoon paprika
3 tablespoons sugar
½ cup olive oil

2 tablespoons butter
¾ cup blanched slivered almonds
  (about 3 ounces)
1 10-ounce bag ready-to-use
  spinach leaves
2 medium-size red-skinned apples,
  quartered, cored, thinly sliced

Combine onion, cider vinegar, white wine vinegar, sesame seeds and paprika in small bowl. Mix in 2 tablespoons sugar. Gradually whisk in olive oil. Season dressing to taste with salt and pepper.

Melt butter in heavy large skillet over medium heat. Add almonds. Stir until almonds begin to color, about 2 minutes. Sprinkle remaining 1 tablespoon sugar over. Stir until sugar melts and begins to turn golden, about 2 minutes longer. Transfer almonds to bowl and cool. (*Dressing and almonds can be prepared 4 hours ahead. Cover separately and let stand at room temperature.*)

Combine spinach and apples in large bowl. Toss with enough dressing to coat. Mix in almonds. Serve salad, passing any remaining dressing separately.

SPICE UP YOUR SALAD

Sun-dried apples are at the core of the smoky, sweet flavor of American Spice vinegar from Sumptuous Selections in Connecticut; cinnamon, cloves and nutmeg round out the recipe. The whole spices retain their zip for a year, so later on you can refill the 200-ml bottle with cider vinegar. Call 800-789-4679.

Watercress, Pear and Walnut Salad with Poppy Seed Dressing

Toasted walnuts add crunch and flavor to this terrific salad.

8 SERVINGS

3 tablespoons apple cider vinegar
4 teaspoons Dijon mustard
1 tablespoon honey
¾ cup corn oil
1 teaspoon poppy seeds

2 large bunches watercress, trimmed
⅔ cup walnuts, toasted, chopped
2 pears, peeled, cut into ¾-inch pieces

Whisk vinegar, mustard and honey in small bowl to blend. Gradually whisk in oil. Mix in poppy seeds. Season dressing to taste with salt and pepper.

Toss watercress and walnuts in large bowl with enough dressing to coat. Season with salt and pepper. Divide salad among 8 plates. Toss pears with ¼ cup dressing in small bowl. Spoon pears atop salads.

Spinach-Orange Salad

Jicama, avocado and red onion take this crisp and colorful salad beyond the ordinary.

8 SERVINGS

½ cup fresh orange juice
¼ cup sherry wine vinegar
3 tablespoons honey
1 tablespoon fresh lime juice
¾ teaspoon chili powder
¾ cup olive oil

2 6-ounce packages baby spinach
4 oranges, peel and white pith removed, quartered, cut crosswise into ¼-inch-thick slices
2 cups matchstick-size strips peeled jicama
1 avocado, peeled, seeded, cubed
½ cup chopped red onion
¼ cup chopped fresh cilantro

Whisk fresh orange juice, sherry wine vinegar, honey, fresh lime juice and chili powder in large bowl to blend. Gradually whisk in olive oil. Season dressing to taste with salt and pepper.

Combine remaining ingredients in another large bowl. Toss salad with enough dressing to coat lightly.

Grain & Pasta Salads

MEDITERRANEAN COUSCOUS SALAD WITH ROASTED VEGETABLES

This meatless salad combines couscous with roasted eggplant, zucchini, red bell pepper and leeks. Cooked sausage may be added to make it heartier.

6 SERVINGS

1 1- to 1¼-pound eggplant, cut lengthwise into 8 wedges

2 medium-size zucchini, each cut lengthwise into 4 wedges

3 large leeks (white and pale green parts only), halved lengthwise, cut crosswise into 2½-inch pieces

1 red bell pepper, cut into ½-inch-wide strips

10 large garlic cloves, unpeeled

3½ tablespoons plus ¼ cup olive oil

2 tablespoons balsamic vinegar

1 tablespoon chopped fresh thyme

1 tablespoon chopped fresh rosemary

2½ cups water

1 teaspoon salt

1 10-ounce box couscous

1 cup pitted brine-cured black olives (such as Kalamata), halved

6 tablespoons fresh lemon juice

3 tablespoons drained capers

3 tablespoons thinly sliced fresh basil

Preheat oven to 400°F. Divide first 5 ingredients between 2 heavy large baking sheets. Brush vegetables with 3 tablespoons oil and balsamic vinegar. Sprinkle herbs over. Sprinkle with salt and pepper. Roast until tender, turning occasionally, about 45 minutes. Cool. Remove and discard peels from garlic. Coarsely chop garlic. Cut roasted vegetables into ¾-inch pieces. Set aside.

Bring 2½ cups water, 1 teaspoon salt and ½ tablespoon oil to boil in medium saucepan. Stir in couscous. Remove from heat. Cover; let stand until water is absorbed, about 5 minutes. Fluff couscous with fork. Transfer to large bowl.

Gently mix roasted garlic and vegetables, ¼ cup oil, olives, lemon juice, capers and basil into couscous. Season with salt and pepper. (*Can be made 1 day ahead. Cover and refrigerate. Let stand 30 minutes at room temperature before serving.*)

Layered Rice Salad with Red and Green Salsas

You'll need a big glass bowl or a trifle dish to show off the salad to its best advantage.

12 SERVINGS

RICE

5½ cups water
 1 tablespoon plus 1 teaspoon
   olive oil
1½ teaspoons salt
 2 cups long-grain white rice

GREEN SALSA

 9 tomatillos,* husked, coarsely
   chopped
1½ cups chopped green bell peppers
 ¾ cup chopped green onions
   (dark green parts only)
 ½ cup chopped fresh basil
 2 tablespoons olive oil

BEANS

 2 15-ounce cans black beans,
   drained, rinsed

 2 teaspoons ground coriander
 1 teaspoon onion salt

RED SALSA

 1 cup purchased medium-hot
   red salsa
 2 cups chopped red bell peppers
 ½ cup chopped red onion
 ⅓ cup chopped fresh parsley
 1 tablespoon olive oil

 1 cup sour cream
 3 tablespoons thinly sliced fresh
   basil

FOR RICE: Combine water, olive oil and salt in large saucepan. Bring to boil. Add rice. Return to boil. Reduce heat to low. Cover saucepan and cook until liquid is absorbed and rice is tender, about 20 minutes. Fluff rice with fork. Transfer to baking sheet and cool completely. Season to taste with salt and pepper.

FOR BEANS: Mix beans, coriander and onion salt in medium bowl.

FOR GREEN SALSA: Combine all ingredients in large bowl. Toss to blend. Season to taste with salt and pepper.

FOR RED SALSA: Mix purchased salsa, bell peppers, onion, parsley and oil in another large bowl. Season to taste with salt and pepper.

Spoon 2 cups rice into 4-quart clear glass bowl. Spoon green salsa evenly over rice. Spoon another 2 cups rice evenly over salsa. Spread sour cream over rice. Spoon all but ¼ cup beans over sour cream. Spread remaining rice over beans. Spread red salsa over rice. Sprinkle remaining ¼ cup beans over salad. Cover and refrigerate at least 1 hour or up to 8 hours. Sprinkle with basil.

A green tomato-like vegetable with a paper-thin husk. Available at Latin American markets and some supermarkets.

GRILLED-VEGETABLE PASTA SALAD WITH PARSLEY VINAIGRETTE

For extra eye appeal, use tricolor pasta in this fresh-from-the-garden salad.

6 SERVINGS

- 1 cup coarsely chopped fresh Italian parsley
- 3 tablespoons red wine vinegar
- 1 large garlic clove
- ½ cup plus 2 tablespoons olive oil (preferably extra-virgin)
- ¾ pound fusilli pasta
- 1 cup hickory smoke chips, soaked in water 30 minutes, drained
- 2 large ears fresh corn, husked
- 2 large zucchini, trimmed, halved lengthwise
- 1 large red onion sliced into 3 large rounds

Blend parsley, vinegar and garlic in processor until parsley is finely chopped, scraping down sides of bowl twice. With machine running, gradually add ½ cup olive oil. Season vinaigrette to taste with salt and pepper.

Cook pasta in large pot of boiling salted water until just tender but still firm to bite, stirring occasionally. Drain pasta. Rinse under cold water and drain again. Transfer to large bowl. Mix in 2 tablespoons vinaigrette.

Prepare barbecue (medium heat). Place smoke chips in 8x6-inch foil packet with open top. Set packet atop coals about 5 minutes before grilling.

Brush corn, zucchini and onion with remaining 2 tablespoons oil. Sprinkle with salt and pepper. Grill vegetables until cooked through and beginning to brown, turning often, about 12 minutes. Cool slightly. Cut kernels from corncobs. Cut zucchini and onion into ½-inch pieces.

Add corn kernels, zucchini and onion to pasta in large bowl. Mix in enough vinaigrette to coat. Season to taste with salt and pepper. *(Can be prepared 8 hours ahead. Cover and refrigerate. Bring to room temperature before serving.)*

PENNE, SPINACH, ASPARAGUS AND CASHEW SALAD

This inventive salad is a terrific addition to any summer buffet.

12 SERVINGS

- 1½ pounds asparagus spears, ends trimmed, cut into 1-inch pieces
- 1½ pounds penne or rigatoni pasta
- 1 tablespoon plus ½ cup olive oil
- ¾ cup sliced green onions
- 6 tablespoons white wine vinegar
- 2 tablespoons soy sauce
- 1 6-ounce package baby spinach
- 1 cup (about 4½ ounces) salted roasted cashews, coarsely chopped

Cook asparagus in large pot of boiling salted water until just tender, about 3 minutes. Using slotted spoon, transfer asparagus to small bowl. Cool. Add pasta to same pot and cook until just tender but still firm to bite. Drain well. Transfer pasta to very large bowl. Toss with 1 tablespoon oil. Cool.

Blend ½ cup oil, green onions, vinegar and soy sauce in blender until smooth, about 2 minutes. (*Asparagus, pasta and dressing can be prepared 1 day ahead. Cover separately; chill.*) Pour dressing over pasta. Add asparagus, spinach and cashews; toss to coat. Season with salt and pepper.

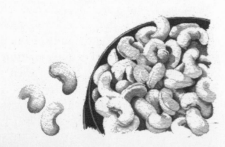

A SCREEN FOR GRILLING GREENS

If you want to grill vegetables and keep them from falling onto the coals, the best thing to do is to buy a grilling rack. Some have grates that run both horizontally and vertically, creating square openings that are too small to let vegetables or delicate foods, such as fish, fall through. Others are made from metal sheets that have small holes punched out. Either way, the racks can be placed right on top of the grill (those with handles are easier to use).

Grilling racks are sold in cookware stores and barbecue specialty shops, or order one by mail from Char-Broil's *Grill Lover's Catalog*. To request a catalog or to order a grilling rack, call 800-241-8981.

Seafood Salads

THAI-STYLE SEAFOOD SALAD WITH HERBS

The seafood is cooked in lime juice and fish sauce, making this oil-free salad perfect for a low-fat appetizer.

8 APPETIZER SERVINGS

1 stalk lemongrass* or 1 tablespoon grated lemon peel

14 ounces cleaned uncooked squid, tentacles reserved, bodies cut into ½-inch-thick rings

8 ounces uncooked large shrimp, peeled, deveined

3 tablespoons fresh lime juice

2 tablespoons fish sauce (nam pla)*

½ teaspoon dried crushed red pepper

½ cup minced shallots

3 tablespoons chopped fresh tarragon

2 tablespoons chopped fresh cilantro

8 crisp lettuce leaves

Discard all but bottom 4 inches of lemongrass stalk. Peel off outer layers from stalk; discard. Thinly slice lemongrass.

Combine squid tentacles and bodies, shrimp, lime juice, fish sauce, crushed red pepper and lemongrass in heavy large skillet. Sauté over medium-high heat until squid and shrimp are just opaque, about 3 minutes. Transfer seafood mixture to medium bowl. Cool completely. Add shallots, tarragon and cilantro to seafood mixture. Season to taste with salt and pepper. Chill until cold, at least 45 minutes or up to 2 hours.

Arrange lettuce leaves on platter. Using slotted spoon, divide squid mixture among lettuce leaves. Spoon some of juices over each salad and serve.

Available at Asian markets and in some supermarkets.

LAYERED PICKLED HERRING SALAD WITH TART APPLES AND RED ONION

One of the layers in this delicious salad is lightly pickled sweet-and-sour cucumbers, a favorite throughout Denmark. They do need to marinate overnight, so make sure you start this recipe a day ahead of time.

8 SERVINGS

CUCUMBERS

¾ cup apple cider vinegar
¾ cup water
⅓ cup sugar
2 teaspoons pickling spice
1 teaspoon salt
1 large hothouse cucumber, cut
    into ½-inch-thick rounds

SALAD

1 pound Granny Smith apples,
    peeled, cored, coarsely chopped
1½ cups chopped red onion
1 cup sour cream
¼ cup chopped fresh dill

1¼ cups sliced trimmed radishes
2 6-ounce jars spiced cut herring,
    drained, each piece halved

Boston lettuce leaves
Fresh dill sprigs (optional)

FOR CUCUMBERS: Mix vinegar, water, sugar, pickling spice and salt in heavy medium saucepan: bring to boil, stirring until sugar and salt dissolve. Cool to room temperature. Place cucumbers in large glass bowl. Pour marinade over cucumbers. Cover; refrigerate overnight.

FOR SALAD: Mix apples, red onion, sour cream and chopped dill in large bowl. Season to taste with salt and pepper.

Using slotted spoon, remove cucumbers from marinade. Arrange half of cucumbers in bottom of 8x8x2-inch glass dish. Arrange half of radishes atop cucumbers. Spoon half of apple mixture over radishes. Arrange herring evenly atop apple mixture. Spoon remaining apple mixture over herring. Cover with remaining cucumbers, then radishes.

Cover and chill salad 3 hours.

Arrange lettuce leaves on platter. Spoon salad onto leaves. Garnish with dill sprigs, if desired, and serve.

Smorgasbord Salad with Smoked Salmon and Dill Sauce

Serve this variation of a traditional Swedish salad with thin slices of buttered pumpernickel bread and small glasses of vodka or aquavit.

4 SERVINGS

¼ cup Dijon mustard
2 tablespoons white wine vinegar
1 tablespoon sugar
1 teaspoon dry mustard
⅓ cup vegetable oil
¼ cup chopped fresh dill

½ small head cabbage, shredded
1 hothouse cucumber, thinly sliced
2 large tomatoes, cut into wedges
1 15-ounce can pickled beet slices, drained
6 ounces thinly sliced smoked salmon
Additional chopped fresh dill

Mix first 4 ingredients in bowl. Gradually mix in oil. Add ¼ cup dill. Season with pepper. *(Can be made 2 days ahead. Chill.)*

Spread cabbage over large platter. Arrange cucumber slices around outer edge of platter. Arrange tomatoes around upper and lower edges of platter, placing just inside cucumber and leaving space at ends. Mound beets at both ends of platter. Place salmon in center. Spoon some sauce over salmon. Sprinkle salmon with dill. Serve, passing remaining sauce.

Salads with Meat

CURLY ENDIVE SALAD WITH WARM BACON DRESSING

The dressing is based on an old Pennsylvania Dutch recipe.

6 SERVINGS

3 tablespoons sugar
1 tablespoon all purpose flour
3 tablespoons plus 1 teaspoon
    apple cider vinegar
1 large egg
1 cup canned vegetable broth,
    low-salt chicken broth or water
6 bacon slices, cut into 1-inch pieces

1 large head curly endive or other
    bitter lettuce (such as escarole),
    torn into bite-size pieces

Combine sugar and flour in small bowl. Gradually whisk in vinegar, then egg. Whisk in broth.

Cook bacon in heavy large skillet over medium heat until crisp and brown. Whisk in vinegar mixture. Stir until dressing comes to simmer and thickens. Season dressing to taste with salt and pepper. (*Can be prepared 1 hour ahead. Let stand at room temperature. Rewarm over low heat before continuing.*)

Place endive in large bowl. Toss with enough dressing to coat. Serve, passing remaining dressing separately.

SWEET-AND-SOUR SPINACH SALAD WITH BACON

6 SERVINGS

2 tablespoons ketchup
2 tablespoons red wine vinegar
4 teaspoons sugar
1 teaspoon Worcestershire sauce
½ cup olive oil
½ cup finely chopped onion

6 bacon slices
1 10-ounce package ready-to-use
    spinach leaves

Whisk ketchup, vinegar, sugar and Worcestershire sauce in small bowl to blend. Gradually whisk in oil; mix in onion. Season dressing to taste with salt and pepper. (*Can be prepared 1 day ahead. Cover and refrigerate.*)

Cook bacon in heavy large skillet over medium heat until brown and crisp. Transfer bacon to paper towels; drain. Crumble bacon. Combine spinach and bacon in large bowl. Toss salad with enough dressing to coat lightly. Divide salad among plates. Serve, passing any remaining dressing separately.

POTATO, CELERY AND HAM SALAD WITH TARRAGON

A dish from the Pays de Caux region in northern France, where it is called salade Cauchoise. The salad is traditionally bound with crème fraîche, but it is delicious made with mayonnaise, too.

4 SERVINGS

1 pound medium-size red-skinned potatoes
1 tablespoon tarragon white-wine vinegar
2¼ cups thinly sliced celery (about 5 stalks)
4 ounces Black Forest ham, cut into 1½x¼-inch strips
6 tablespoons mayonnaise or crème fraîche
3 tablespoons chopped fresh tarragon
Fresh tarragon sprigs (optional)

Cook potatoes in large pot of boiling salted water until just tender, about 22 minutes. Drain. Cool to lukewarm. Peel potatoes. Cut into ½-inch-thick slices and place in large bowl. Drizzle vinegar over; toss to coat. Cool completely.

Add celery, ham, mayonnaise and chopped tarragon to potatoes; toss gently. Season with salt and pepper. Garnish with tarragon sprigs, if desired.

ARUGULA WITH PROSCIUTTO AND MANGO

In this easy salad, salty prosciutto contrasts with peppery arugula and cooling mango.

4 SERVINGS

2 mangoes, peeled, pitted, cubed
2 tablespoons dry Marsala

4 teaspoons extra-virgin olive oil
2 teaspoons sherry wine vinegar
4 large bunches arugula, torn
1 tablespoon freshly grated Parmesan
12 paper-thin prosciutto slices

Combine mangoes and Marsala in medium bowl. Chill until cold, about 1 hour.

Mix oil and vinegar in large bowl. Add arugula and cheese; toss to coat. Season with salt and pepper. Divide arugula among 4 plates. Place 3 prosciutto slices around arugula on each plate. Spoon mangoes and any juice in center.

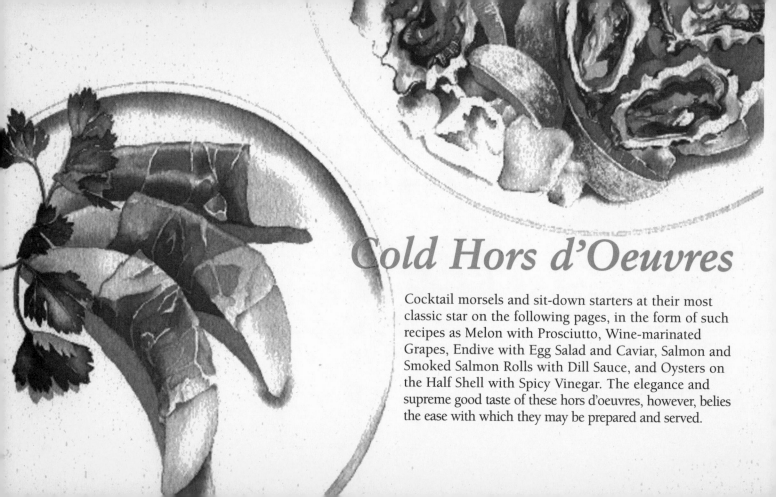

Cold Hors d'Oeuvres

Cocktail morsels and sit-down starters at their most classic star on the following pages, in the form of such recipes as Melon with Prosciutto, Wine-marinated Grapes, Endive with Egg Salad and Caviar, Salmon and Smoked Salmon Rolls with Dill Sauce, and Oysters on the Half Shell with Spicy Vinegar. The elegance and supreme good taste of these hors d'oeuvres, however, belies the ease with which they may be prepared and served.

Vegetables

MARINATED RED PEPPERS WITH ANCHOVIES

6 SERVINGS

2 large red bell peppers
1 2-ounce can anchovies
2 tablespoons chopped fresh Italian parsley
1 tablespoon chopped fresh oregano or 1 teaspoon dried
1 tablespoon olive oil
2 teaspoons red wine vinegar

Arugula or escarole leaves
Breadsticks

Char red bell peppers over gas flame or in broiler until blackened on all sides. Wrap in paper bag and let stand 10 minutes. Peel and seed bell peppers. Cut peppers into ½- to ¾-inch-thick strips. Place in small bowl. Add anchovies and their oil. Mix in parsley, oregano, olive oil and red wine vinegar. Season mixture with pepper. Let marinate at room temperature at least 30 minutes. (*Can be prepared 2 days ahead. Cover tightly and refrigerate. Bring to room temperature before serving.*)

Line plates with arugula. Top with pepper mixture. Serve with breadsticks.

VEGGIE SNACKS

Crispy, light and all-natural. Sound like a great potato chip? Actually, it's a description of Veggibles, a snack that has the added benefit of being very nutritious. Each 1.2-ounce package of freeze-dried carrots, peas, red bell peppers and corn has only one gram of fat and six grams of dietary fiber. Plus, the crunchy dried vegetables retain their high concentrations of vitamins A and C. Veggibles come in chili-lime, barbecue and teriyaki flavors. They are made by Beverly Hills Farmers Market and can be found in supermarkets and natural foods stores.

ARTICHOKE BOTTOMS WITH CRÈME FRAÎCHE AND CAVIAR

Using canned artichokes makes this appetizer a cinch to assemble. The basil and lemon add a refreshing flavor to the creamy filling.

6 SERVINGS

⅓ cup crème fraîche or sour cream
3 tablespoons chopped green onions (green part only)
2½ tablespoons chopped fresh basil
1 teaspoon grated lemon peel

6 canned artichoke bottoms, drained (pat dry)
1 2-ounce jar salmon caviar
Fresh basil sprigs

Mix first 4 ingredients in small bowl. Season with salt and pepper. (*Filling can be made 1 day ahead. Cover and refrigerate.*)

Spoon filling onto artichokes. Top each with 1 teaspoon caviar. Garnish with fresh basil sprigs.

Fruit

Wine-marinated Grapes

Mix some chilled club soda into the leftover wine marinade for a refreshing drink.

6 TO 8 SERVINGS

1 750-ml bottle dry white wine
(such as Fumé Blanc)
¼ cup plus 3 tablespoons sugar
2 pounds red and/or green seedless
grapes, cut into small clusters
1 tablespoon grated lemon peel

Pour wine into large nonaluminum bowl. Add ¼ cup sugar and stir until dissolved. Add grapes and peel; mix gently. Cover; chill at least 3 hours and up to 1 day.

Using slotted spoon, transfer grapes to shallow bowl. Sprinkle grapes with remaining 3 tablespoons sugar and serve.

Melon and Lox with Chives and Lemon

This simple appetizer is a clever blend of sweet, salty and tangy flavors.

4 SERVINGS

½ small to medium honeydew
melon, peeled, seeded, sliced
4 ounces thinly sliced lox
3 tablespoons chopped fresh chives
8 thin lemon wedges

Divide melon slices among plates. Top with lox. Sprinkle chives over. Season to taste with pepper. Place 2 lemon wedges on each plate and serve.

Melon with Prosciutto

The delicate pink cured ham from the hills of the province of Parma is one of Emilia's most important products. Purists insist it should be served on its own or with a slice of bread, but others enjoy it with melon, figs or pears–the sweetness of the fruit sets off the prosciutto's salty tinge perfectly. This simple dish is a classic example.

6 SERVINGS

1 melon, cut into 6 wedges
18 paper-thin prosciutto slices

Place 1 melon wedge on each of 6 plates. Arrange 3 prosciutto slices alongside melon or drape over melon and serve.

Eggs

DEVILED EGGS WITH SUN-DRIED TOMATOES AND CHIVES

MAKES 10

6 large hard-boiled eggs, shelled
¼ cup finely chopped drained
   oil-packed sun-dried tomatoes
¼ cup minced fresh chives
1 tablespoon olive oil
1½ teaspoons minced fresh thyme
1 teaspoon white wine vinegar
   Additional drained oil-packed
   sun-dried tomatoes, cut into strips

Cut eggs lengthwise in half. Scoop yolks into medium bowl. Mash yolks coarsely with fork. Finely chop 2 egg white halves; mix into yolks. Add chopped sun-dried tomatoes and next 4 ingredients; mix well. Season with salt and pepper. Spoon about 1 tablespoon filling into each egg half, mounding slightly. Top with tomato strips. (*Can be made 8 hours ahead. Cover; chill.*)

PSEUDO SUN-DRIED TOMATOES

Drying tomatoes in the sun is only recommended in areas that have very low humidity and very high temperatures (like parts of the Mediterranean or the Southwest). But you can oven-dry tomatoes in any climate and achieve virtually the same results as you would by sun-drying them.

Start with ripe plum tomatoes (beef-steak, cherry and other varieties have too much water). Wash and dry the tomatoes, then slice them in half lengthwise and scrape out the seeds. You may lightly salt the tomatoes if you'd like (in order to draw out the water), but be careful not to oversalt because the final product should be sweet.

Preheat the oven to a very low temperature, about 170°F. Arrange the halved tomatoes skin side down on racks placed on baking sheets. Place the sheets in the oven, and prop open the oven door with a wooden spoon to improve air circulation. Check the tomatoes every hour or so; the smaller ones will dry faster than the larger ones, which could take 12 hours or more to dry thoroughly. As they dry, the tomatoes will shrivel and darken; they'll begin to feel like leather.

After all the tomatoes have been dried and removed from the oven, store them in airtight containers or pack them in jars filled with olive oil (make sure the tomatoes are completely covered by the oil, and store them in the refrigerator; otherwise they might mold). Dried tomatoes will keep for up to a year.

Endive with Egg Salad and Caviar

6 SERVINGS

6 tablespoons mayonnaise
1 tablespoon Dijon mustard
8 hard-boiled eggs, peeled, chopped
¼ cup finely chopped onion
¼ cup finely chopped celery
¼ cup chopped fresh basil

1 ounce caviar
24 Belgian endive spears

Mix mayonnaise and mustard in bowl. Mix in eggs, onion, celery and basil. Season with salt and pepper. Cover; chill until ready to serve or up to 6 hours ahead.

Place egg salad on platter. Garnish with caviar. Surround with endive spears.

Seafood

Poached Trout with Horseradish-Dill Sauce

6 SERVINGS

3 cups water
1 cup apple cider vinegar
¾ cup chopped fresh dill
3 tablespoons fresh lemon juice
2 18-ounce trout, cleaned

1 cup mayonnaise
½ cup sour cream
3 tablespoons prepared horseradish

Assorted crackers and sliced bread
Radishes

Combine water, vinegar, ½ cup dill and lemon juice in heavy large skillet. Bring to boil. Add trout; cover and simmer until cooked through, about 8 minutes. Using slotted spatula, transfer trout to platter. Cover and refrigerate trout until cold, about 3 hours.

Mix 1 cup mayonnaise, ½ cup sour cream, 3 tablespoons prepared horseradish and remaining ¼ cup chopped dill in small bowl. Season sauce to taste with salt and pepper. Cover sauce tightly and refrigerate at least 2 hours to develop flavors. (*Trout and sauce can be prepared 1 day ahead. Keep refrigerated.*)

Place sauce on platter. Surround with trout, crackers, bread and radishes.

Salmon and Smoked Salmon Rolls with Dill Sauce
(COVER RECIPE)

8 SERVINGS

1 1½-pound center-cut salmon fillet

6 large zucchini (each about 7 inches long and 1½ inches thick), trimmed

1½ cups mayonnaise

¾ cup plus 3 tablespoons chopped
    fresh dill
7 teaspoons white wine vinegar

6 ounces smoked salmon (not lox),
    coarsely chopped
3 tablespoons chopped dill pickle

Sprinkle salmon with salt and pepper. Steam until just opaque in center, about 15 minutes. Cool completely.

Line baking sheet with paper towels. Slice enough ⅛-inch-thick lengthwise strips from center portion of each zucchini to make 24. Steam in batches until just tender but very pliable, about 3 minutes. Transfer to prepared baking sheet; pat dry.

Whisk mayonnaise, ¾ cup dill and vinegar in small bowl. Season dill sauce to taste with salt and pepper.

Flake salmon coarsely into large bowl, discarding skin and bones. Gently mix in smoked salmon, pickle, remaining 3 tablespoons dill and ¼ cup dill sauce.

Place 1 rounded tablespoon salmon mixture at end of each zucchini strip. Roll up strips, enclosing salmon. Place rolls seam side down on platter. (*Can be made 1 day ahead. Place rolls on paper towels. Cover rolls and sauce separately; chill.*)

Serve rolls with remaining dill sauce.

Oysters on the Half Shell with Spicy Vinegar

12 SERVINGS

1½ cups apple cider vinegar
 1 teaspoon salt
½ cup very thinly sliced green onions
⅓ cup finely chopped shallots
 5 garlic cloves, minced
 2 teaspoons coarsely ground
    black pepper
¼ cup finely chopped fresh parsley

36 fresh oysters, on the half shell
    Lemon wedges

Stir vinegar and salt in medium bowl until salt dissolves. Mix in green onions, shallots, garlic and black pepper. Let stand at room temperature 30 minutes. Season to taste with additional salt, if desired. (*Can be prepared 2 days ahead. Cover and refrigerate.*) Stir parsley into vinegar mixture.

Line platter with crushed ice. Arrange oysters atop ice. Spoon 1 teaspoon vinegar mixture over each oyster. Transfer remaining vinegar mixture to small bowl. Serve oysters with lemon wedges and remaining vinegar mixture.

BEST SHELLER

The "April" oyster shucker from Mepra is a pearl of a utensil. Six inches long, it has an easy-to-grasp blue handle and a hefty blade that makes quick work of manipulating mollusks. Call Fillamento at 415-931-2224 to place an order.

SHRIMP AND CRAB CEVICHE WITH AVOCADO

While this refreshing seafood appetizer is now made in most of Central and South America, it was born in Peru, and to this day cooks there are acknowledged as the masters of the dish. In a classically prepared ceviche, the always-present citrus juice is used to "cook" and flavor the seafood; in this inventive recipe, the juice is used just to flavor cooked shellfish.

6 SERVINGS

½ pound plum tomatoes, halved, seeded
1 large red bell pepper, halved, seeded
1 large jalapeño chili, halved, seeded
1 medium (about 10 ounces) white onion, peeled, cut into 6 wedges
6 tablespoons fresh lime juice
2 tablespoons fresh orange juice
1 tablespoon ketchup
1 teaspoon prepared white horseradish
½ teaspoon hot pepper sauce (such as Tabasco)

1 pound cooked large shrimp, peeled, deveined, cut in half lengthwise
½ cup chopped tomato
½ cup chopped fresh cilantro
1 green onion, chopped
1 ripe avocado, halved, pitted, peeled
½ pound crabmeat, drained, picked over

Preheat broiler. Place tomato halves, bell pepper and jalapeño, skin side up, on baking sheet. Place onion on baking sheet. Broil vegetables until slightly blackened, about 5 minutes. Transfer vegetables to blender. Add lime juice and next 4 ingredients. Blend until almost smooth. Transfer sauce to large bowl. Season with salt and pepper. Refrigerate until cold. (*Can be prepared 1 day ahead. Cover and keep chilled.*)

Add shrimp to sauce. Mix in chopped tomato, cilantro and green onion. Cube 1 avocado half. Slice other half. Fold avocado cubes and crab into ceviche. Garnish with avocado slices and serve.

Hot Appetizers

Fragrant, flavorful and beguiling in their contrasts
of texture, hot appetizers are often the mst popular
part of a cocktail buffet. From Crunchy Fried
Shrimp with Cayenne Aioli to Spinach-Bacon Roll-ups,
Pan-Asian Spareribs to Orange-scented Crab Cakes
with Fresh Tomato Relish, these finger foods are sure to
delight your guests. Yet, with much of the preparation
done in advance, they make work incomparably simple
for the host or hostess as well.

Vegetables & Cheese

MELTED SWISS CHEESE WITH VEGETABLES

In this simplified version of raclette, one of Switzerland's classic dishes, Swiss cheese replaces raclette cheese, and the cheese is melted in individual portions instead of being scraped from a large wheel as it melts.

6 APPETIZER SERVINGS

12 baby red-skinned potatoes

3 large carrots, peeled, cut into ¾-inch pieces

4 cups broccoli florets (from 2 large stalks)

2 red bell peppers, cut into 1-inch squares

1 15-ounce can whole beets, drained

1 4- to 5-ounce jar cocktail onions, drained

1 15- to 18-inch-long baguette, sliced

1½ pounds thinly sliced Swiss cheese

Preheat oven to 350°F. Cook potatoes in large pot of boiling salted water 8 minutes. Add carrots and boil 7 minutes. Add broccoli and boil until all vegetables are tender, about 3 minutes longer. Drain vegetables. Arrange potatoes, carrots, broccoli, bell peppers, beets and onions on large platter. Place bread in basket.

Divide sliced cheese among 6 ovenproof plates. Bake until cheese melts and bubbles, about 10 minutes. Serve with vegetables and bread.

YAM CHIPS

The yams sold in markets here are actually red-skinned sweet potatoes. To ensure a crisp chip in this recipe, make sure to slice the yams very thinly.

6 TO 8 SERVINGS

2 pounds yams

Canola oil (for deep-frying)

Peel yams. Using large sharp knife, carefully slice yams crosswise into paper-thin (1-millimeter) rounds.

Pour oil into heavy medium saucepan to depth of 3 inches and heat to 325°F. Working in batches, fry yam slices until they begin to curl and brown in spots, stirring occasionally, about 3 minutes. Using slotted spoon, transfer chips to paper towels; drain. Season with salt. Transfer to serving bowl. Serve warm or at room temperature. (*Can be made 3 hours ahead.*)

CLASSIC SAGANAKI WITH OLIVES AND LEMON
(COVER RECIPE)

Saganaki, *pan-fried rectangles of a hard cheese such as* kasseri *or* kefalotyri, *are standard ouzerie fare and a beloved accompaniment to–you guessed it–ouzo. The specialty gets its name from the two-handled pan in which it is made, but it can be prepared in any heavy small skillet. For a final flourish, the cheese is often splashed with ouzo and flamed. Tomato wedges, olives and pita bread are the recommended go-withs here.*

4 TO 6 SERVINGS

1 8-ounce package kasseri cheese*
or Pecorino Romano, cut into
½-inch-thick rectangular slices

All purpose flour
3 tablespoons (about) olive oil

½ lemon
1 tablespoon chopped fresh oregano
Tomato wedges
Pita wedges

Kalamata olives

Rinse cheese slices under cold water (do not pat dry). Coat with flour. Heat oil in heavy large skillet over medium-high heat until almost smoking. Add cheese and cook until beginning to brown, about 1 minute per side. Transfer to plates.

Squeeze lemon over cheese; sprinkle with oregano and pepper. Serve with tomatoes, pita and olives.

*A firm sheep's-milk cheese. Available at Greek markets and many supermarkets.

BRIE, PAPAYA AND ONION QUESADILLAS

These versatile quesadillas can be passed as hors d'oeuvres, or offered at dinner as a first course or at lunch as the entrée.

MAKES 4

1 tablespoon olive oil
½ large onion, thinly sliced
2 to 3 teaspoons minced seeded
jalapeño chili

8 6-inch-diameter flour tortillas
8 ounces Brie, diced
½ cup chopped fresh cilantro
½ large papaya, peeled, seeded,
thinly sliced crosswise

Sour cream
Purchased salsa (optional)

Preheat oven to 425°F. Heat oil in medium skillet over medium-high heat. Add onion and jalapeño and sauté until onion is just tender, about 4 minutes; cool slightly.

Arrange 4 tortillas on heavy large baking sheet. Arrange Brie, then cilantro, papaya and onion mixture over tortillas, dividing equally. Top each with another tortilla, pressing to adhere.

Bake quesadillas until cheese melts and filling is heated through, about 8 minutes. Transfer quesadillas to plates; cut into wedges. Serve, passing sour cream and salsa, if desired.

WHOLE WHEAT CREPES WITH CORN, BELL PEPPER AND CHEESE FILLING

Cooking crepes can be tricky, so don't hesitate to practice the techniques a couple of times–this recipe allows for extras.

6 SERVINGS

CREPES
1 cup low-fat (1%) milk
2 large eggs
⅓ cup water
½ teaspoon salt
⅔ cup whole wheat pastry flour*
⅓ cup unbleached all purpose flour

2 tablespoons (¼ stick) butter, melted

FILLING
1 tablespoon olive oil
1 cup chopped onion
1¼ cups finely diced red bell pepper
2 teaspoons minced garlic
1¾ cups fresh corn kernels

1 teaspoon chopped fresh rosemary or ½ teaspoon dried
1 teaspoon chopped fresh thyme or ½ teaspoon dried
1 cup nonfat cottage cheese
⅓ cup (about 2 ounces) soft fresh goat cheese (such as Montrachet)
3 tablespoons grated Pecorino Romano cheese
2 large egg whites (unbeaten)

Red Bell Pepper Puree (see recipe)

FOR CREPES: Blend milk, eggs, water and salt in blender. With machine running, add both flours in 4 additions total. Blend 1 minute. Transfer batter to medium bowl. Refrigerate 2 hours.

Heat medium nonstick skillet with 6½-inch-diameter bottom over medium-high heat. Lightly brush bottom of pan with some of melted butter. Whisk batter to blend well. Add 2 tablespoons batter to pan and swirl pan to coat bottom thinly. Cook until edges are brown and crepe lifts easily, about 45 seconds. Loosen edges of crepe gently with spatula. Carefully turn crepe over; cook until beginning to brown in spots, about 20 seconds. Turn crepe out onto plate. Place paper towel atop crepe. Repeat with remaining crepe batter, using 2 tablespoons per crepe, brushing pan with melted butter as needed and covering each crepe with paper towel. (*Can be made 1 day ahead. Wrap crepes layered between paper towels tightly in foil and chill.*)

FOR FILLING: Heat oil in large nonstick skillet over medium heat. Add onion and sauté until tender, about 4 minutes. Add bell pepper and garlic; sauté until bell pepper is tender, about 5 minutes. Add corn kernels, rosemary and thyme; sauté until corn is heated through, about 5 minutes longer. Season with salt and pepper. Cool completely.

Blend cottage cheese and goat cheese in processor until smooth. Transfer to large bowl. Stir in corn mixture and Romano cheese. Season filling to taste with salt and pepper. Mix in egg whites. (*Can be prepared 3 hours ahead; chill.*)

Preheat oven to 400°F. Lightly butter 13x9x2-inch glass baking dish. Spoon generous 2 tablespoons filling down center of each crepe. Roll up crepes. Arrange crepes, seam side down, in prepared baking dish. Cover with foil. Bake until heated through, about 20 minutes. Spoon Red Bell Pepper Puree over crepes and serve.

Also called whole grain pastry flour. Available at most natural foods stores and some supermarkets.

RED BELL PEPPER PUREE

Prepare this one day ahead so that its rich flavor can develop.

MAKES ABOUT 2 CUPS

5 red bell peppers (about 2 pounds)

1 tablespoon olive oil
2 garlic cloves, minced

2 tablespoons low-fat buttermilk
¼ teaspoon sugar

Preheat oven to 450°F. Place bell peppers on baking sheet. Bake until puffed and blackened on all sides, turning every 10 minutes, about 30 minutes. Transfer to large bowl; cover with plate. Let stand 30 minutes. Peel, stem and seed peppers over medium bowl to collect juice. Transfer peppers to processor. Strain accumulated bell pepper juice into small bowl; reserve.

Heat oil in small nonstick skillet over medium-low heat. Add garlic; sauté until just golden, about 30 seconds. Transfer garlic and oil to processor with peppers. Puree. Add buttermilk and sugar. Season with salt and pepper; thin with reserved bell pepper juice, if desired. Transfer to small bowl; serve warm or at room temperature. (*Can be made 1 day ahead. Chill. Bring to room temperature before serving.*)

BELL PEPPERS FILLED WITH CAPERS, OLIVES, ANCHOVIES, RAISINS AND PINE NUTS

This classic starter highlights many of the distinctive flavors of southern Italian cooking.

6 APPETIZER SERVINGS

3 medium-size red bell peppers
3 medium-size yellow bell peppers

2 tablespoons raisins
1 cup fresh breadcrumbs from French bread
¼ cup brine-cured black olives (such as Gaeta or Kalamata), pitted, chopped
3 tablespoons pine nuts, toasted
3 tablespoons chopped fresh basil
3 tablespoons chopped fresh Italian parsley
2 tablespoons drained capers, chopped
2 medium garlic cloves, minced
2 anchovy fillets, minced

½ teaspoon (scant) salt
5 tablespoons olive oil

Lightly oil 13x9-inch baking dish. Char peppers over gas flame or in broiler until blackened on all sides but not soft. Wrap in paper bag and let stand 10 minutes. Peel peppers. Cut lengthwise in half. Cut out stems and scrape out seeds. Arrange peppers, cut side up, in single layer in prepared dish.

Preheat oven to 350°F. Place raisins in small bowl. Add enough hot water to cover. Let stand 10 minutes. Drain raisins; chop coarsely. Place in medium bowl. Add breadcrumbs and next 8 ingredients; toss to combine. Season with pepper. Mix in 3 tablespoons oil. Spoon into peppers. Drizzle 2 tablespoons oil over. (*Can be made 6 hours ahead. Cover and chill.*) Bake until peppers are heated through but still hold their shape, about 30 minutes. Serve hot or at room temperature.

Seafood

COCONUT-LIME SHRIMP WITH PEANUT SAUCE

4 SERVINGS

PEANUT SAUCE

⅓ cup creamy peanut butter (do not use old-fashioned style or freshly ground)
¼ cup canned low-salt chicken broth
2 tablespoons canned unsweetened coconut milk*
1 teaspoon fresh lime juice
1 teaspoon soy sauce
1 teaspoon fish sauce (nam pla)**
1 teaspoon hot pepper sauce (such as Tabasco)

SHRIMP

1 cup coarsely chopped fresh basil
½ cup canned unsweetened coconut milk
1½ tablespoons finely chopped garlic

1½ tablespoons fresh lime juice
1 tablespoon minced peeled fresh ginger
2 teaspoons soy sauce
2 teaspoons fish sauce (nam pla)
2 teaspoons golden brown sugar
20 large shrimp, peeled, deveined

1 cup hickory smoke chips, soaked in water 30 minutes, drained
4 bamboo skewers, soaked in water 30 minutes, drained

FOR PEANUT SAUCE: Puree all ingredients in processor until smooth. (*Can be prepared 1 day ahead. Cover and refrigerate. Bring to room temperature before using.*)

FOR SHRIMP: Blend first 8 ingredients in processor until almost smooth. Transfer marinade to 13x9x2-inch glass baking dish. Add shrimp and turn to coat. Cover and refrigerate 2 hours, turning occasionally.

Prepare barbecue (medium-high heat). Place smoke chips in 8x6-inch foil packet with open top. Set atop coals. Thread 5 shrimp onto each of 4 skewers. Grill until just cooked through, basting with marinade, about 2 minutes per side.

Serve shrimp with peanut sauce.

*Available at Indian, Asian or Latin American markets and many supermarkets.

**Available at Asian markets and in the Asian section of many supermarkets.

CRUNCHY FRIED SHRIMP WITH CAYENNE AIOLI

This starter gets a double dose of cayenne–in the cornmeal coating for the shrimp and in the garlicky mayonnaise dip.

6 APPETIZER SERVINGS

1⅓ cups regular or low-fat
    mayonnaise
2½ teaspoons fresh lemon juice
 2 garlic cloves, pressed
 1 teaspoon cayenne pepper
½ teaspoon Dijon mustard

Peanut oil (for frying)
½ cup yellow cornmeal
½ teaspoon salt

1½ pounds uncooked jumbo shrimp,
    peeled, deveined

Whisk mayonnaise, lemon juice, garlic, ½ teaspoon cayenne and mustard in small bowl to blend. (*Can be made 1 day ahead. Cover tightly with plastic wrap; refrigerate.*)

Pour enough oil in heavy large pot to reach depth of 2 inches; heat to 375°F. Mix cornmeal, salt and ½ teaspoon cayenne in medium bowl. Add shrimp to bowl; toss to coat. Working in batches, add shrimp to hot oil and deep-fry until shrimp are golden and opaque in center, about 1½ minutes. Using slotted spoon, transfer shrimp to paper towels to drain.

Place aioli in center of platter; surround with shrimp and serve.

CONCERNING CAYENNE

While some recipes still call for "ground red pepper, preferably cayenne," most of what is labeled "cayenne" these days is actually a blend of several types of ground dried red chilies that need not contain any cayenne at all. (Fresh cayenne peppers *are* available at Latin American markets.)

Pure cayenne does actually have a flavor, despite its heat (on a scale of 10, the cayenne falls somewhere between 7 and 8); Santa Fe chef Mark Miller praises its pungent, tart, smoky taste. The trick is managing to get enough of it on your tongue to evaluate such nuances without actually passing out. This is probably a good time to note that once chilies have been dried and ground, neither their fire nor their flavor lasts long. The best way to preserve both is by storing your jar of cayenne in a cool, dark place; replace any unused spice every six months or so.

Orange-scented Crab Cakes with Fresh Tomato Relish

MAKES ABOUT 20

TOMATO RELISH

2 teaspoons balsamic vinegar
1 teaspoon golden brown sugar
¼ cup chopped shallots
1 cup diced seeded plum tomatoes
1 tablespoon fresh orange juice
¼ teaspoon dried crushed red pepper
1½ tablespoons chopped fresh parsley

CRAB CAKES

4½ tablespoons mayonnaise
1 large egg
1 tablespoon grated orange peel
1 teaspoon Dijon mustard
½ teaspoon salt
¼ teaspoon cayenne pepper
1 pound fresh crabmeat, picked over, drained
1 cup fresh breadcrumbs
3 tablespoons finely chopped green onion
1 tablespoon chopped fresh parsley
⅓ cup all purpose flour
1 tablespoon (or more) butter
1 tablespoon (or more) vegetable oil

FOR TOMATO RELISH: Whisk vinegar and sugar in medium skillet over medium heat until sugar dissolves. Add shallots; stir just until tender, about 2 minutes. Add tomatoes, orange juice and red pepper; stir until heated through. Remove from heat. Mix in parsley. Season with salt and pepper. (*Can be made 4 hours ahead. Chill. Bring to room temperature before using.*)

FOR CRAB CAKES: Blend mayonnaise, egg, orange peel, mustard, salt and cayenne in large bowl. Stir in crabmeat, breadcrumbs, green onion and parsley. Using 2 tablespoons of mixture for each cake, form twenty 2-inch-diameter cakes. Place on baking sheet. Cover; chill 1 hour. (*Can be made 1 day ahead. Keep chilled.*)

Place flour in small bowl. Lightly coat each crab cake with flour. Melt 1 tablespoon butter with 1 tablespoon oil in heavy large skillet over medium heat. Add crab cakes in batches; cook until golden, adding more butter and oil if necessary, about 5 minutes per side. Arrange on platter. Spoon some relish atop each crab cake. Serve immediately.

Steamed Mussels with Tomatoes and Garlic Toasts

To debeard the mussels, just pull off the hairlike bits coming out from the shell.

8 SERVINGS

8 ½-inch-thick slices sourdough bread (each about 2x4 inches)
6 tablespoons olive oil
4 tablespoons chopped garlic

1½ cups chopped seeded plum tomatoes
½ cup chopped fresh Italian parsley
3 pounds mussels, scrubbed, debearded

Preheat oven to 375°F. Arrange bread on baking sheet. Combine 4 tablespoons oil and 2 tablespoons garlic in bowl. Using fork, mash to coarse paste. Spread over bread. Bake until crisp, about 10 minutes.

Heat 2 tablespoons oil in heavy large pot over medium-high heat. Add 2 tablespoons garlic; sauté 2 minutes. Add tomatoes and parsley. Reduce heat; simmer until sauce thickens, stirring often, about 10 minutes. Season with salt and pepper. Add mussels; increase heat to high. Cover; cook until mussels open, about 7 minutes (discard any mussels that do not open).

Divide mussel mixture among soup bowls. Place toasts at edge of each bowl.

FISHY BUSINESS

Health Sea has tapped the icy blue waters of Alaska to offer an extensive line of their Keta brand smoked wild salmon products. Along with salmon bagel spread and salmon ham, there are salmon sausages in six flavors, including sun-dried tomato and basil, fire-roasted chili pepper, and honey and apple. The items, which are made from naturally lean salmon fillets, are 99 percent fat free (except for the spread) and light on the cholesterol.

Keta products are available in some supermarkets.

Meats

SPINACH-BACON ROLL-UPS

A perfect accompaniment for cocktails. Most of the prep work here can be done ahead.

MAKES ABOUT 30

6 bacon slices
1 10-ounce package frozen chopped spinach, thawed, squeezed dry
4 ounces cream cheese, room temperature
¼ cup mayonnaise
1 teaspoon salt
½ teaspoon pepper
½ cup chopped green onions

3 9-inch-diameter flour tortillas

Cook bacon in heavy large skillet over medium heat until crisp; drain. Crumble bacon into medium bowl; stir in spinach and next 5 ingredients.

Heat 1 tortilla in large skillet over high heat until warm and pliable, about 1 minute per side. Transfer to work surface. Spread ⅓ of filling over tortilla, leaving ½-inch border. Roll up tightly, enclosing filling. Wrap in plastic. Repeat with remaining 2 tortillas and filling. Chill until filling is firm, at least 1 hour or up to 4 hours.

Preheat oven to 400°F. Remove plastic; slice off unfilled ends. Cut rolls crosswise on slight diagonal into ¾-inch-thick slices. Arrange on large baking sheet. Bake until heated through, about 7 minutes.

QUESO FUNDIDO WITH SAUSAGE AND CHIPOTLE CHILIES

This Mexican first course–normally made with a mild, stringy local cheese–is particularly popular in and around Guadalajara, in the central state of Jalisco. There it is called queso fundido *(literally, "melted cheese").*

The chipotles are our own device; if you like more heat, add another teaspoon of the chilies. Offer purchased salsa alongside.

4 SERVINGS

½ pound hot Italian sausages, casings removed
1¾ cups chopped onion
1 cup chopped fresh cilantro
2 teaspoons chopped canned chipotle chilies*
10 ounces Monterey Jack cheese, grated (about 2½ cups packed)

12 6-inch-diameter flour or corn tortillas

Preheat oven to 350°F. Sauté sausages and onion in large skillet over medium-high heat until brown, breaking up clumps of sausage with back of spoon, about 10 minutes. Mix in ½ cup cilantro and 1 teaspoon chipotle chilies. Transfer mixture to 9-inch-diameter baking dish. Mix cheese and remaining ½ cup cilantro and 1 teaspoon chipotle chilies in medium bowl. Sprinkle cheese mixture over sausage mixture. Bake casserole 10 minutes.

Wrap tortillas in aluminum foil. Place tortillas in oven to heat through. Continue to bake casserole until cheese bubbles, about 10 minutes.

Serve casserole with warm tortillas.

Canned chipotle chilies in adobo sauce are available at Latin American markets and most supermarkets.

PAN-ASIAN TERIYAKI SPARERIBS

4 SERVINGS

2 3-pound racks pork spareribs, trimmed

1 12-ounce bottle thick teriyaki baste and glaze
⅓ cup dry sherry
4 teaspoons dark brown sugar
1 tablespoon finely chopped peeled fresh ginger
1½ teaspoons chili-garlic sauce*

1 cup hickory smoke chips, soaked in water 30 minutes, drained

Position rack in middle of oven and preheat to 375°F. Sprinkle ribs with pepper. Wrap each rib rack tightly with heavy-duty foil. Set packets on large rimmed baking sheet. Bake ribs until just tender, about 1 hour 15 minutes. Cool ribs 30 minutes in foil. Unwrap foil. Pour all juices from ribs into medium bowl. (*Can be made 1 day ahead. Cover ribs and pan juices separately and chill.*)

Spoon off and discard fat from surface of pan juices. Stir teriyaki baste and next 4 ingredients into pan juices.

Prepare barbecue (medium heat). Place smoke chips in 8x6-inch foil packet with open top. Set packet atop coals about 5 minutes before grilling. Grill ribs until heated through and well glazed, turning and basting often with teriyaki mixture, about 20 minutes total.

Available at Asian markets and in the Asian section of many supermarkets.

Bruschette, Pizzas, Pastries & Breads

Some of the simplest and most satisfying starters begin with nothing more than a slice of bread or a ball of dough. Add a topping and heat it up, however, and you get extraordinarily tempting results like Tomato and Mozzarella Bruschette, Ham Toasts with Corn and Bell Pepper Relish, Three-Onion Tart with Taleggio, or Pizza with Caramelized Onions, Blue Cheese and Mushrooms. And don't forget the great breads that conclude this chapter. They make wonderful companions to other appetizers and hors d'oeuvres.

Bruschette, Crostini & Toasts

SUN-DRIED TOMATO AND BRIE TOASTS

These Brie cheese toasts are ideal for entertaining. They're easy to prepare, and they make an elegant hors d'oeuvre for a crowd.

MAKES ABOUT 35

1 10-ounce wedge chilled Brie
1 7.5-ounce jar sun-dried tomatoes (packed in oil), drained
1 French bread baguette

⅓ cup olive oil
2 large garlic cloves, minced

⅓ cup pine nuts
3 tablespoons fresh chopped basil

Cut all rind off cheese. Place tomatoes in food processor. Using on/off turns, puree tomatoes until almost smooth. Transfer to small bowl. Cut baguette diagonally into ¾-inch-thick slices. *(Can be made 1 day ahead. Cover; refrigerate cheese and tomato puree separately. Store bread in sealable plastic bag at room temperature.)*

Preheat oven to 325°F. Combine oil and garlic in small bowl. Place bread slices on baking sheet. Lightly brush bread with garlic-oil mixture. Bake until bread is warmed through, about 5 minutes. Remove from oven; maintain temperature.

Spread 1 teaspoon tomato puree evenly over top of each bread slice. Using sharp knife, cut Brie into ⅛-inch-thick slices. Top toasts with cheese. Bake 2 minutes. Remove from oven and sprinkle with pine nuts. Bake until cheese melts, about 5 minutes longer. Transfer toasts to platter; sprinkle with basil and serve.

TOASTY COUSINS

Both bruschette and crostini are slices of toasted country bread topped with flavorful ingredients and served as appetizers. The secret is the toasting; Bruschette are grilled; crostini are baked.

After grilling, bruschette are generally rubbed with olive oil and raw garlic cloves. The bread may then be simply sprinkled with salt and pepper, or topped with a variety of mixtures, the most popular being chopped tomatoes and basil.

Crostini are usually brushed with olive oil and sometimes rubbed with garlic *before* they are baked. Most toppings–including the classic one, chicken liver pâté–are added after baking, but sometimes (especially if one of the ingredients is cheese) they'll be added before.

OLIVE-ONION PUFFS

These flavorful toasts are easy enough to make for last-minute guests.

MAKES ABOUT 25

1 cup chopped pitted black olives,
    drained (about 4 ounces)
½ cup grated Parmesan cheese
½ cup mayonnaise
2 green onions, finely chopped
1 sourdough baguette, cut crosswise
    on slight diagonal into ½-inch-
    thick slices

Preheat broiler. Stir olives, cheese, mayonnaise and onions in small bowl to blend. Season with salt and pepper. Mound 1 tablespoon olive mixture on each bread slice. Arrange on baking sheet. Broil until topping is heated through and begins to brown, about 2 minutes. Serve hot.

TOMATO AND BASIL BRUSCHETTE

MAKES 24

12 6x2x½-inch-thick slices country
    bread, cut crosswise in half
6 tablespoons olive oil
3 garlic cloves, peeled

2 pounds tomatoes, seeded,
    cut into ⅓-inch pieces
¼ cup chopped fresh basil

Preheat oven to 375°F. Arrange bread slices on large baking sheet. Brush bread with 3 tablespoons oil. Bake until bread is toasted and golden brown, about 10 minutes. Rub toasts with garlic.

Mix tomatoes, basil and remaining 3 tablespoons oil in bowl. Season to taste with salt and pepper. Spoon 2 tablespoons tomato topping on each toast. Arrange on platter and serve.

TOMATO AND MOZZARELLA BRUSCHETTE

12 SERVINGS

12 4½x2½-inch slices (each ¾-inch-
    thick) crusty French bread
2 garlic cloves, halved
3 tablespoons olive oil
2 teaspoons balsamic vinegar
1 8-ounce ball fresh mozzarella
    cheese, cut into twelve ¼-inch-
    thick slices
24 ¼-inch-thick slices plum tomatoes
12 fresh basil leaves

Preheat broiler. Broil bread until brown, about 1 minute per side. Rub cut side of garlic over bread. Mix oil and vinegar in small bowl. Brush mixture over bread. Top each bread slice with 1 slice of cheese, 2 tomato slices and 1 basil leaf. Sprinkle with salt and pepper and serve.

MOZZARELLA

For most Italians, mozzarella means only *mozzarella di bufala*, which is made from the milk of water buffalo. True, there exists a type of mozzarella called *fior di latte* that is made from cow's milk and is useful for reasons of economy, but it lacks the luscious characteristics of the original.

Americans have only recently had access to genuine mozzarella di bufala, imported from Italy and available in good cheese shops within a day or two of its manufacture in Battipaglia, south of Naples, and in Caserta, just to the north. But for generations Italian-American neighborhood grocers have been selling their own fior di latte, more often called simply *mozzarella*. To make it, each morning fresh cow's-milk cheese curds are stretched in hot water; then the mass is shaped into balls and braids called *trecce*. This stretching of the curd is the critical act in mozzarella making, for it gives the cheese the springy texture and layered structure that are so desirable.

Along with texture, however, goes taste, and that's where buffalo's-milk mozzarella really comes into its own. True mozzarella is a complex cheese with a decided tang and a fragrance of lactic acid, along with what Italians like to call a "mossy" aroma that they say comes from the marshy ponds in which the buffalo graze.

Imported mozzarella is usually sold in a double plastic bag filled with brine or plain water. If you have a choice, buy mozzarella packed in brine, and return any unused cheese to the brine before storing it in the refrigerator.

You can recognize a good mozzarella by its thin, glossy skin; springy texture; porcelain color; and fresh, milky aroma. If the skin is at all yellow or the cheese has a sour smell, it's over the hill and not worth buying.

WILD MUSHROOM BRUSCHETTE

MAKES 24

12 6x2x½-inch-thick slices country
   bread, cut crosswise in half
 8 tablespoons olive oil

1½ pounds mixed fresh wild
   mushrooms (such as chanterelle,
   stemmed shiitake, portobello
   and/or oyster), thinly sliced
14 garlic cloves, thinly sliced
1½ cups dry white wine
 ½ cup chopped fresh mint

Preheat oven to 375°F. Arrange bread slices on large baking sheet. Brush bread with 3 tablespoons oil. Bake until bread is toasted, about 10 minutes.

Heat 5 tablespoons oil in large skillet over low heat. Add mushrooms and garlic; sauté 5 minutes. Increase heat to high. Add wine; bring to boil. Reduce heat and simmer until almost all liquid evaporates, stir-ring occasionally, about 20 minutes. Season with salt and pepper. Mix in mint. (*Can be made 2 hours ahead. Let toasts and mushrooms stand at room temperature.*)

Spoon mushrooms over toasts.

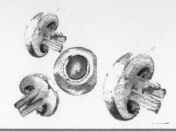

PONDERING PORTOBELLOS

Portobello mushrooms do have an Italian-sounding name, but no one is sure why. They're grown in America, and the bulk of the ones you see in the supermarket are from Pennsylvania.

Though they seem exotic, the richly flavored fungi are actually just common brown button mushrooms left to grow a few extra days. This explains their large size—easily up to six inches in diameter.

Portobellos have been well known in America only for about ten years, although they have been around much longer. For decades, these mushrooms have been quietly enjoyed by Italian-American farmers in Pennsylvania, which may be how they acquired their Italian-sounding moniker. It is assumed that the name was chosen as a marketing ploy to make the ungainly mushroom seem more glamorous.

Walnut, Arugula and Gorgonzola Crostini

In this easy starter, a mix of tangy blue cheese, chopped toasted walnuts and peppery arugula makes a delicious topping for baguette toasts.

6 SERVINGS

Butter, room temperature
18 ¼-inch-thick diagonal baguette
 bread slices

6 tablespoons chopped toasted
 walnuts
3 ounces Gorgonzola cheese,
 crumbled
3 tablespoons finely chopped
 arugula
 Arugula leaves

Preheat oven to 400°F. Spread butter over 1 side of each baguette slice. Arrange baguette slices on baking sheet, butter side up. Bake baguette slices until golden, about 12 minutes. Cool.

 Reduce oven temperature to 350°F. Mix walnuts, Gorgonzola and arugula in medium bowl. Spoon nut-cheese mixture evenly atop baguette toasts, pressing to adhere. Season toasts with pepper. Bake toasts just until cheese melts, about 6 minutes. Cool crostini slightly. Arrange crostini on platter. Garnish platter with arugula leaves and serve.

Ham Toasts with Corn and Bell Pepper Relish

MAKES 36

3 tablespoons vegetable oil
1 cup chopped red onion
1 cup chopped red bell pepper
2 cups frozen corn kernels, thawed

3 tablespoons apple cider vinegar
1 tablespoon (packed) golden
 brown sugar
2½ teaspoons dried thyme
1½ teaspoons dry mustard
1 teaspoon salt
3 generous pinches of cayenne
 pepper

¼ cup (½ stick) butter, room
 temperature
9 slices firm whole grain bread,
 toasted
8 ounces thinly sliced Black Forest
 ham

Heat oil in heavy large skillet over medium-high heat. Add onion and red bell pepper; sauté 5 minutes. Add corn and sauté until vegetables are tender, about 3 minutes longer. Remove from heat.

 Whisk vinegar, sugar, thyme, dry mustard, salt and cayenne in small bowl. Add mixture to vegetables. Return skillet to medium-high heat; cook until liquid evaporates, stirring occasionally, about 4 minutes. Remove from heat. Season with salt and pepper. Transfer to bowl; cool. (*Can be made 1 day ahead. Cover and chill. Bring to room temperature before using.*)

 Spread butter over 1 side of each toast. Divide ham among toasts, trimming edges to fit. Cut each toast into 4 triangles. Place triangles on platter. Spoon some relish atop each triangle and serve.

CROSTINI WITH SPICED CRAB AND SHRIMP SALAD

A nice do-ahead starter for an elegant meal.

MAKES 40

½ cup bottled clam juice
10 ounces medium uncooked
    shrimp, peeled, deveined
2 cups thinly sliced green onions
⅔ cup mayonnaise
4 teaspoons fresh lemon juice
2 garlic cloves, finely chopped
1 teaspoon Hungarian sweet paprika
½ teaspoon cayenne pepper
8 ounces flaked crabmeat (about
    2 cups lightly packed)

⅓ cup (about) olive oil
40 ¼-inch-thick diagonal slices
    sourdough baguette

Lemon wedges

Bring clam juice to simmer in large skillet over medium heat. Add shrimp; cover and simmer until opaque, turning once, about 2 minutes. Using slotted spoon, transfer shrimp to cutting board; coarsely chop shrimp. Place shrimp in small bowl. Boil cooking liquid until reduced to 2 tablespoons, about 2 minutes. Cool.

Mix onions and next 5 ingredients in large bowl to blend. Stir in shrimp, cooking liquid and crabmeat. Season with salt and pepper. Cover and chill.

Preheat oven to 375°F. Lightly brush oil over both sides of each bread slice. Arrange bread on baking sheet in single layer. Bake until bread is crisp and golden, about 4 minutes per side. Cool. *(Seafood salad and toasts can be made 1 day ahead. Keep seafood salad chilled. Store toasts airtight at room temperature.)*

Spread seafood salad evenly over toasts. Arrange on serving dish. Garnish with lemon wedges and serve.

Pizzas

TOMATO-MOZZARELLA PIZZA WITH PHYLLO CRUST

Crispy phyllo takes the place of a traditional pizza crust in this inventive recipe, which is a great appetizer.

MAKES 15 PIECES

6 tablespoons (¾ stick) butter,
    melted
8 sheets fresh phyllo pastry or
    frozen, thawed
8 tablespoons grated Parmesan
    cheese
6 ounces shredded mozzarella
    cheese (about 1¾ cups)
1 medium onion, thinly sliced
1½ pounds plum tomatoes, halved,
    seeded, sliced into rounds
1 teaspoon dried oregano
½ teaspoon dried thyme

Preheat oven to 375°F. Brush 15x10x1-inch baking sheet with butter. Place 1 phyllo sheet in prepared pan (edges of phyllo may go up sides of baking sheet). Brush phyllo with butter; sprinkle with 1 tablespoon Parmesan cheese. Repeat layering with remaining phyllo, butter and Parmesan cheese. Top with even layers of mozzarella cheese and onion, then tomatoes. Sprinkle with oregano and thyme.

Bake until crust is crisp and golden brown at edges, cheese melts and tomatoes are tender, about 30 minutes. Let stand 5 minutes.

Cut pizza into squares and serve hot.

PIZZA WITH CARAMELIZED ONIONS, BLUE CHEESE AND MUSHROOMS

Sweet caramelized onions, tangy blue cheese and meaty shiitake mushrooms team up perfectly in this meatless pizza.

MAKES 1 LARGE PIZZA

2½ tablespoons olive oil
2 large onions, thinly sliced
  (about 5 cups)
2 teaspoons brown sugar

8 ounces fresh shiitake mushrooms, stemmed, caps sliced
1 12-inch-diameter baked cheese pizza crust (such as Boboli)
8 ounces blue cheese, crumbled
1 tablespoon chopped fresh thyme or 1 teaspoon dried

Heat 1 tablespoon oil in large nonstick skillet over medium heat. Add onions and sauté until tender, about 10 minutes.

Sprinkle brown sugar over onions. Reduce heat to medium-low; sauté until onions are golden brown, about 20 minutes.

Heat 1½ tablespoons oil in large skillet over high heat. Add mushrooms; sauté until tender and golden, about 8 minutes. Season with salt and pepper. (*Onions and mushrooms can be prepared 1 day ahead. Cover separately and refrigerate.*)

Preheat oven to 450°F. Place pizza crust on large baking sheet. Sprinkle blue cheese and thyme over pizza crust. Top with onions. Sprinkle mushrooms over.

Bake pizza until cheese melts, about 15 minutes. Cool pizza in pan 5 minutes. Cut into wedges.

MEXICAN PIZZA WITH CHORIZO, MONTEREY JACK CHEESE AND SUN-DRIED TOMATOES

Tortillas form the crust of these layered piz-zas, which are an irresistible hors d'oeuvre.

12 SERVINGS

2 ounces sun-dried tomatoes
(do not use oil-packed)
4 tablespoons plus 2 teaspoons
olive oil
2 tablespoons balsamic vinegar

¾ pound pork chorizo, casings
removed

1 garlic clove, minced
4 9-inch flour tortillas
1½ cups grated Monterey Jack cheese
4 teaspoons pine nuts, toasted
2 teaspoons dried oregano

1 poblano chili,* sliced into 12 rings

Place tomatoes in medium bowl. Add enough boiling water to cover; steep until soft, about 15 minutes. Drain tomatoes. Slice tomatoes into matchstick-size strips and place in small bowl. Add 2 tablespoons oil and vinegar; toss to coat. Season to taste with salt and pepper. (*Tomatoes can be prepared 1 day ahead. Cover and let stand at room temperature.*)

Line baking pan with paper towels. Cook chorizo in large nonstick skillet over medium heat until brown, crumbling with back of fork, about 10 minutes. Using slotted spoon, transfer chorizo to prepared baking pan to drain.

Preheat oven to 350°F. Lightly oil baking sheet. Drain tomatoes, reserving vinaigrette. Sprinkle garlic over 2 tortillas. Sprinkle ¼ of cheese, ¼ of chorizo, ¼ of sun-dried tomatoes, 1 teaspoon pine nuts and 1 teaspoon oregano atop each. Place remaining 2 tortillas atop pizzas. Heat 1 tablespoon plus 1 teaspoon oil in large skillet over medium heat. Place 1 pizza in skillet and cook until golden brown on bottom, about 4 minutes. Turn pizza, bottom side up, onto prepared baking sheet. Repeat with remaining oil and pizza.

Sprinkle remaining cheese, chorizo and sun-dried tomatoes equally atop pizzas. Place 6 poblano chili rings atop each pizza. Brush reserved vinaigrette over chili rings. Sprinkle remaining 2 teaspoons pine nuts over pizzas. Bake pizzas until bottoms are brown and cheese melts, about 10 minutes. Transfer pizzas to cutting board. Cut each pizza into 12 wedges and serve.

A fresh green chili, often called a passilla, available at Latin American markets and some supermarkets.

PIZZA WITH FETA, TOMATOES AND SHRIMP

Purchased baked pizza crusts are a delicious alternative to making your own pizza dough. This Greek-inspired pie is prepared with robust Mediterranean ingredients–tomatoes, feta cheese, olives and oregano.

MAKES 1 LARGE PIZZA

1 12-inch-diameter baked cheese pizza crust (such as Boboli)

8 ounces mozzarella cheese, grated (about 2 cups packed)

1 pound plum tomatoes, thinly sliced

8 ounces feta cheese, crumbled

16 brine-cured black olives (such as Kalamata), pitted

½ cup chopped green onions (green part only)

2 tablespoons chopped fresh oregano or 2 teaspoons dried

½ pound cooked peeled large shrimp

Preheat oven to 450°F. Place pizza crust on baking sheet. Sprinkle mozzarella over. Arrange tomatoes atop cheese. Sprinkle feta over tomatoes. Sprinkle olives, ⅓ cup green onions and oregano over pizza.

Bake pizza 10 minutes. Remove pizza from oven. Arrange shrimp atop pizza. Continue baking until crust is golden and mozzarella melts, about 4 minutes longer. Cool pizza in pan 5 minutes. Sprinkle remaining green onions over pizza. Cut into wedges and serve.

PIZZA WITH FONTINA, PEPPERONI AND TOMATOES

Fontina cheese gives this all-time favorite a richer taste, and dried crushed red pepper gives it a spicy kick.

MAKES 1 LARGE PIZZA

1 12-inch-diameter baked cheese pizza crust (such as Boboli)

8 ounces Fontina cheese, grated (about 2 cups packed)

2½ ounces pepperoni, thinly sliced

4 large plum tomatoes, chopped (about 1½ cups)

2 tablespoons chopped fresh sage or 1½ teaspoons dried rubbed sage

½ teaspoon dried crushed red pepper

Preheat oven to 450°F. Place crust on large baking sheet. Sprinkle Fontina over. Arrange pepperoni atop cheese. Sprinkle tomatoes, sage and red pepper over pizza. Season lightly with salt.

Bake pizza until crust is golden and cheese melts, about 15 minutes. Cool in pan 5 minutes. Cut into wedges.

Pastries

THREE-ONION TART WITH TALEGGIO

8 SERVINGS

CRUST

2¾ cups all purpose flour
¼ teaspoon salt
1 large egg, beaten to blend
1½ tablespoons olive oil
6 tablespoons (¾ stick) unsalted butter, melted, cooled
⅓ cup cold milk

TOPPING

3½ cups thinly sliced leeks (white and pale green parts only; about 2 medium)
3 tablespoons extra-virgin olive oil
1 large red onion, thinly sliced
1 cup sliced green onions
1 large egg, beaten to blend

8 ounces Taleggio cheese, cut into small pieces
2 tablespoons grated Parmesan cheese

FOR CRUST: Mix flour and salt in large bowl. Make well in center of flour mixture. Add egg and oil to well. Pour melted butter and milk into well. Mix ingredients in well, gradually incorporating flour until dough forms. Turn dough out onto floured surface and knead until smooth, about 10 minutes. Form into ball. Wrap in kitchen towel; let stand at room temperature 2 hours.

FOR TOPPING: Combine leeks and oil in large nonstick skillet. Cover and cook over medium-low heat until leeks are tender but not brown, stirring frequently, about 15 minutes. Stir in red onion and green onions. Sauté uncovered until all onions are very tender, about 25 minutes longer. Season with salt and pepper. Cool. Mix in egg, then Taleggio cheese.

Preheat oven to 375°F. Roll out dough on floured surface, forming 13-inch round. Transfer to large rimless baking sheet. Fold outer 1 inch of dough over, forming double-thick rim. Spread topping evenly over crust. Bake tart 10 minutes. Sprinkle Parmesan over. Bake until crust is golden, about 15 minutes longer. Cut into wedges.

TALEGGIO

Soft, buttery Taleggio has a characteristic flat, square shape and, with age, an amber-colored rind. It's made from the milk of Holstein and Brown Swiss cows that are grazed on lush, spring-fed pastures in the northern part of Lombardy–in the Taleggio Valley, in fact–although there is limited production of Taleggio in both Piedmont and Veneto as well.

This is one of a group of cow's-milk cheeses that Italians refer to collectively as *stracchino*. You might see Taleggio sold by that name, although the cheese's DOC trademark–a clover-like shape enclosing stylized, linked letters, with the producer's number embossed on the top–is unmistakable. Stracchino cheeses were traditionally made from the milk of so-called "tired" cows–*stracch*, in the Lombard dialect. Their milk, after the stress of the long journey between high Alpine summer pastures and lower winter grazing lands, was extra rich in butterfat. Stracchino cheeses are fine in their own right, but Taleggio, with its complex flavor, is truly the apotheosis of the type.

Taleggio is a washed-rind cheese, meaning exactly what it says: Once the cheese has been formed, it is kept in a warm, humid environment and washed with salted water regularly over a period of five to six weeks while the cheese ages. The finest Taleggio is still ripened, according to tradition, in cold mountain caves, but modern industrial producers use refrigerated storerooms instead.

This is a cheese of many nuances. The interior of a young Taleggio is the color of pale straw; the texture is soft without being runny, springy without being rubbery. With age, the soft rind develops an orangy-caramel crust, and the cheese becomes even more buttery, with a slight tang and a smokiness that can recall the fragrance of white truffles. That nuance is enhanced quite nicely when the Taleggio is topped with a few drops of truffle oil.

Puff Pastry Turnovers with Shrimp, Scallops and Spinach

MAKES 8

3 tablespoons butter
8 ounces mushrooms, sliced
⅓ cup finely chopped shallots
1 cup whipping cream
½ cup dry white wine
½ cup canned low-salt chicken broth
1½ tablespoons Dijon mustard
1 teaspoon white wine vinegar
1 10-ounce package frozen chopped spinach, thawed, squeezed dry

1 17¼-ounce package frozen puff pastry (2 sheets), thawed
16 uncooked large shrimp, peeled, deveined
8 sea scallops, halved horizontally

Preheat oven to 500°F. Melt butter in heavy large skillet over medium-high heat. Add mushrooms and shallots; sauté 5 minutes. Add cream, wine and broth. Boil until mixture is reduced to 1 cup, about 12 minutes. Mix in mustard and vinegar, then spinach. Season with salt and pepper. Cool.

Roll out 1 pastry sheet on lightly floured surface to 12-inch square. Cut pastry into four 6-inch squares. Place ⅛ of spinach mixture on bottom half of 1 square. Top spinach mixture with 2 shrimp and 2 scallop halves. Brush pastry edges with water. Fold unfilled half of pastry over filling, forming rectangle. Press edges of pastry closed with tines of fork. Place pastry on large baking sheet. Repeat with remaining pastry, spinach mixture, shrimp and scallops.

Bake pastries 5 minutes. Reduce heat to 375°F. Bake pastries until puffed and golden brown, about 15 minutes longer. Serve warm.

Breads, Biscuits & Crackers

Anadama Rolls with Mixed Seeds

Anadama bread recipes, which date back to pre-Revolutionary New England, all call for molasses and cornmeal for substantial–and delicious–results. This contemporary rendition is no exception.

MAKES 16

1½ cups milk (do not use low-fat or nonfat)
⅓ cup mild-flavored (light) molasses
2 tablespoons (¼ stick) unsalted butter
2 teaspoons salt

¼ cup warm water (105°F to 115°F)
2 envelopes dry yeast

¾ cup yellow cornmeal
1½ cups whole wheat flour
2¾ cups (about) bread flour

Additional yellow cornmeal

1 egg, beaten to blend (glaze)
Assorted seeds (such as fennel,
anise, celery and/or caraway)

Mix milk, molasses, butter and salt in small saucepan. Bring to simmer. Pour milk mixture into bowl of heavy-duty mixer fitted with paddle attachment. Cool to 115°F, about 30 minutes.

Meanwhile, place ¼ cup warm water in measuring cup. Sprinkle yeast over and stir to blend. Let stand until yeast dissolves, about 10 minutes. Stir yeast mixture into milk mixture. Mix in ¾ cup cornmeal. Mix in whole wheat flour. Mix in enough bread flour, ½ cup at a time, to form slightly sticky dough. Turn dough out onto floured surface. Knead until smooth and elastic, adding more bread flour if dough is too sticky, about 8 minutes. Form dough into ball.

Butter large bowl. Place dough in bowl; turn to coat. Cover bowl with plastic wrap, then towel. Let dough rise in warm area until doubled, about 1½ hours.

Sprinkle 2 heavy large baking sheets generously with cornmeal. Punch down dough. Turn out onto floured surface and knead until smooth, about 3 minutes. Divide dough into 16 equal portions. Roll each portion between palms and work surface to 8-inch-long rope about ¾ inch thick. Grasping 1 rope at both ends, tie into loose knot. Repeat with remaining ropes. Place on prepared baking sheets, spacing 2 inches apart. Cover with towels. Let rise in warm area until almost doubled, about 45 minutes.

Position 1 rack in center and 1 rack in top third of oven and preheat to 375°F. Brush rolls with egg glaze. Sprinkle with seeds. Bake until rolls are golden and sound hollow when tapped, switching and rotating baking sheets halfway through baking, about 20 minutes. Transfer rolls to racks. (*Can be made 2 weeks ahead. Cool. Wrap in foil; freeze. If desired, rewarm thawed wrapped rolls in 350°F oven 10 minutes.*) Serve warm or at room temperature.

Toasted Jalapeño Corn Bread

Jalapeño chilies give this a nice spicy kick.

MAKES 20 SQUARES

3 tablespoons olive oil
1½ cups chopped onions
¼ cup minced seeded jalapeño chilies

1½ cups yellow cornmeal
1½ cups all purpose flour
1 tablespoon baking powder
2 teaspoons salt
¾ teaspoon baking soda
1½ cups buttermilk
3 large eggs, separated
¼ cup (½ stick) unsalted butter, melted

1 tablespoon plus 1 teaspoon sugar

Preheat oven to 400°F. Generously butter 13x9x2-inch glass baking dish. Heat oil in medium skillet over medium heat. Add onions and jalapeños; sauté until onions are tender, about 5 minutes.

Mix cornmeal, flour, baking powder, salt and baking soda in large bowl. Whisk buttermilk, yolks and butter in medium bowl to blend. Mix buttermilk mixture into dry ingredients just until moist and blended. Stir in onion mixture.

Using electric mixer, beat egg whites in another large bowl until soft peaks form. Add sugar and beat until whites are stiff but not dry. Stir ⅓ of whites into batter to lighten. Fold in remaining whites. Transfer batter to prepared pan. Bake until corn bread is golden and tester inserted into center comes out clean, about 25 minutes. *(Can be prepared 8 hours ahead. Cool; cover with foil and store at room temperature. Rewarm covered in 350°F oven for 10 minutes before serving.)* Cut into 20 squares and serve warm.

Sesame Buttermilk Corn Biscuits with Cheddar Cheese

African slaves smuggled sesame, or benne, seeds into the South and used them to accent soups, cookies and candies, and to coat chicken and fish before frying. Sesame seeds add crunch to delicate sage- and thyme-scented biscuits.

MAKES ABOUT 24

5 tablespoons sesame seeds

2½ cups unbleached all purpose flour
4 teaspoons baking powder
1 tablespoon sugar
¾ teaspoon salt
½ teaspoon baking soda
½ cup yellow cornmeal
½ cup plus 2 tablespoons (1¼ sticks) chilled unsalted butter, cut into ½-inch pieces
1½ cups buttermilk
4 teaspoons chopped fresh sage or

1½ teaspoons dried rubbed sage
1 tablespoon chopped fresh thyme
   or 1 teaspoon dried
2 cups grated extra-sharp cheddar
   cheese (about 7½ ounces)

Additional buttermilk

Position 1 rack in center and 1 rack in top third of oven and preheat to 450°F. Place sesame seeds in heavy small skillet. Stir over medium heat until golden, about 2 minutes. Cool.

Sift flour, baking powder, sugar, salt and baking soda into large bowl. Add yellow cornmeal and 3 tablespoons sesame seeds and stir to blend. Add chilled butter and rub in with fingertips until mixture resembles coarse meal. Whisk 1½ cups buttermilk, chopped sage and thyme in medium bowl to blend. Add to dry ingredients and stir to blend well. Mix in cheese (dough will be slightly sticky). Gather dough into ball.

Turn dough out onto generously floured work surface. Knead dough about 6 to 8 turns, adding more flour if dough is too sticky. Roll out dough to generous ¾-inch thickness. Using 2¼-inch-diameter biscuit or cookie cutter, cut out biscuits. Reroll dough scraps and cut out additional biscuits. Place biscuits on 2 ungreased baking sheets, spacing evenly. Brush biscuits with additional buttermilk. Sprinkle biscuit tops with 2 tablespoons toasted sesame seeds.

Bake biscuits until golden brown, switching and rotating baking sheets halfway through baking, about 16 minutes. Serve biscuits warm. (*Biscuits can be prepared 8 hours ahead. Let stand at room temperature. Rewarm biscuits in 350°F oven just until heated through, about 5 minutes.*)

FLATBREAD WITH ONIONS AND MUSTARD SEEDS

Thanks to purchased frozen dough, this bread is a snap to make. Serve it with soups, salads and pastas.

MAKES 1 FLATBREAD

1 pound frozen white bread dough
   (⅓ of 3-pound package), thawed

3 tablespoons olive oil
3 cups finely chopped onions
2 tablespoons minced garlic
2½ tablespoons Dijon mustard
2 tablespoons yellow mustard seeds
1½ teaspoons dried thyme

Place dough in large bowl. Cover with towel and let rise in warm draft-free area until doubled, about 1 hour.

Preheat oven to 450°F. Heat 2 tablespoons oil in large nonstick skillet over medium heat. Add onions and garlic and sauté until brown and tender, about 10 minutes. Add mustard, mustard seeds and thyme and stir 1 minute. Cool.

Oil large baking sheet. Using rolling pin, roll out dough on floured surface to 14x5-inch rectangle. Spread ⅓ cup onion mixture evenly over dough. Starting at 1 short end, roll up dough jelly roll style. Using rolling pin, roll out dough to 12x8-inch rectangle. Transfer to prepared baking sheet. Brush with remaining 1 tablespoon oil. Sprinkle remaining onion mixture atop dough.

Bake bread until golden brown, about 20 minutes. Serve warm or at room temperature.

Whole Wheat Biscuits with Maple Butter

MAKES ABOUT 15

2 cups whole wheat flour
1 tablespoon plus 1 teaspoon baking powder
1 tablespoon sugar
¾ teaspoon salt
½ teaspoon baking soda
⅓ cup chilled solid vegetable shortening, cut into pieces
1 cup chilled buttermilk

Maple Butter (see recipe)

Preheat oven to 400°F. Mix first 5 ingredients in large bowl. Cut in shortening until mixture resembles coarse meal. Mix in buttermilk. Gather dough into ball. Knead gently on lightly floured surface until dough holds together, about 5 seconds. Pat dough out to ¾-inch thickness. Cut out biscuits, using 2-inch cookie cutter. Gather scraps, pat out and cut more biscuits. Transfer to baking sheet.

Bake biscuits until puffed and golden, about 15 minutes. Cool slightly. (*Can be made 8 hours ahead. Cool. Before serving, wrap in foil; rewarm in 400°F oven for 5 minutes.*) Serve warm with Maple Butter.

Maple Butter

MAKES ABOUT 1 CUP

½ cup (1 stick) unsalted butter, room temperature
1 tablespoon (packed) golden brown sugar
⅛ teaspoon imitation maple flavoring
½ cup pure maple syrup

Blend first 3 ingredients in processor until smooth. With machine running, gradually blend in syrup, stopping occasionally to scrape down sides of bowl. Transfer butter to bowl. (*Can be made 4 days ahead. Chill. Bring to room temperature before using.*)

Spicy Cheese Biscuits

MAKES ABOUT 9 BISCUITS

3½ cups all purpose flour
2 tablespoons baking powder
1 tablespoon sugar
2 teaspoons cayenne pepper
½ teaspoon salt
1 cup grated sharp cheddar cheese
¾ cup grated Romano cheese
⅔ cup chilled vegetable shortening,
   cut into small pieces
1¼ cups chilled buttermilk

Preheat oven to 450°F. Butter large baking sheet. Sift first 5 ingredients twice into medium bowl. Mix in cheeses. Add shortening; rub in with fingertips until mixture resembles coarse meal. Add buttermilk, stirring until dough begins to form clumps.

Turn dough out onto lightly floured surface; knead gently until smooth, about 8 turns. Roll out dough to ¾-inch thickness. Using 3-inch-diameter biscuit cutter, cut out biscuits. Gather dough scraps; roll out to ¾-inch thickness. Cut out additional biscuits. Transfer biscuits to prepared baking sheet. Bake until puffed and golden brown, about 15 minutes. Serve warm.

Jalapeño and Cheddar Cheese Corn Sticks

These also come out very nicely when baked in standard muffin cups.

MAKES 48

5 tablespoons (about) butter, melted
4 cups yellow cornmeal
4 cups all purpose flour
1 cup sugar
¼ cup baking powder
4 teaspoons salt
4 cups whole milk
1⅓ cups vegetable oil
4 large eggs
3 cups grated cheddar cheese
   (about 10 ounces)
¼ cup finely chopped seeded
   jalapeño chilies

Preheat oven to 400°F. Brush 24 ¼-cup corn stick molds or ⅓-cup muffin cups with some of butter. Mix cornmeal and next 4 ingredients in large bowl. Whisk milk, oil and eggs in another large bowl to blend; add cheese and chilies. Mix liquids into dry ingredients. Spoon half of batter into molds. Bake until toothpick inserted into center comes out clean, about 15 minutes. Turn out onto racks. Wipe molds clean. Brush with butter. Fill and bake with remaining batter as described above. (*Can be made 1 day ahead. Cool. Wrap in foil and let stand at room temperature. Rewarm foil-wrapped corn sticks in 400°F oven for 5 minutes.*) Serve warm.

Soft Cornmeal Pretzels with Onions, Mustard and Poppy Seeds

German settlers in eastern Pennsylvania, known as the Pennsylvania Dutch (from Deutsch), brought with them a reverence for big meals; a typical saying was "Better a burst stomach than wasted food." They also brought an Alsatian recipe for pretzels, which became a favorite throughout the region. The tender bread gets its pretty golden color from mustard and its crunchy top from a sprinkling of poppy seeds and coarse salt.

MAKES 16

2 tablespoons (¼ stick) butter
2 cups finely chopped onions

2 cups warm water (105°F to 115°F)
2 envelopes dry yeast
1 tablespoon plus 1 teaspoon sugar

2 tablespoons prepared yellow mustard (such as French's)
1 teaspoon dry mustard
½ cup yellow cornmeal
2½ teaspoons salt
4¾ cups (about) bread flour

Additional yellow cornmeal

12 cups water
2 tablespoons baking soda
1 egg yolk, beaten to blend with
    1 tablespoon water (glaze)
Coarse salt
Poppy seeds

Melt butter in large nonstick skillet over medium-low heat. Add onions and sauté until tender and deep golden, about 15 minutes. Remove from heat and cool.

Pour 1½ cups warm water into large bowl of heavy-duty mixer fitted with paddle attachment. Sprinkle yeast and 1 tablespoon sugar over; stir to blend. Let stand until yeast foams, about 10 minutes.

Whisk remaining ½ cup water, prepared mustard and dry mustard in small bowl to blend. Mix into yeast mixture. Mix in ½ cup cornmeal and 2 teaspoons salt. At low speed, mix in 4½ cups flour, 1 cup at a time. Beat 3 minutes. Add onion mixture and beat just until incorporated (dough will be sticky).

Sprinkle work surface with ¼ cup flour. Turn dough out onto floured surface. Knead dough until smooth and slightly sticky, adding more flour by tablespoonfuls if very sticky, about 8 minutes. Form dough into ball.

Butter large bowl. Add dough and turn to coat. Cover bowl with towel. Let dough rise in warm area until doubled, about 1 hour.

Sprinkle 2 baking sheets with additional yellow cornmeal. Punch dough down. Turn dough out onto floured work surface and knead briefly until smooth. Divide dough into 16 equal pieces. Roll 1 piece between palms and work surface into 15-inch-long rope. To form pretzel, grasp each end of rope and curve center of rope into circle; cross ends twice, fold up over center of circle and press into opposite side of circle to adhere. Place pretzel on prepared baking sheet. Repeat rolling and forming pretzels with remaining dough pieces.

Let pretzels rise uncovered in warm area until almost doubled in volume, about 20 minutes.

Meanwhile, bring 12 cups water to boil in heavy large pot. Position 1 rack in center and 1 rack in top third of oven and preheat to 375°F. Butter 2 clean baking sheets and sprinkle with additional yellow cornmeal.

Add baking soda, remaining 1 teaspoon sugar and remaining ½ teaspoon salt to boiling water in pot (water will bubble up vigorously). Using spatula, transfer 4 pretzels to boiling water and

cook 30 seconds per side. Using same spatula, transfer pretzels to prepared baking sheets, spacing evenly. Repeat with remaining pretzels. Brush boiled pretzels with egg glaze. Sprinkle with coarse salt and poppy seeds.

Bake until pretzels are golden brown, switching and rotating baking sheets halfway through baking, about 20 minutes. Transfer baking sheets to racks and cool

pretzels. (*Can be prepared 2 weeks ahead. Wrap pretzels tightly in aluminum foil and freeze. Rewarm thawed pretzels in 350°F oven about 10 minutes.*)

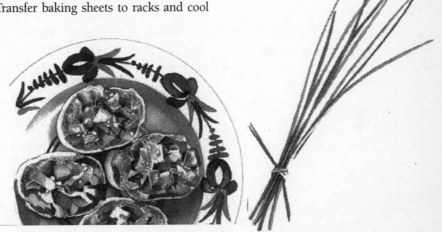

CORN BREAD WITH BACON AND GREEN ONIONS

Crackling corn bread, made with salt pork or pork rinds, was popular in Colonial days. Here's an updated version that uses bacon; corn kernels are mixed in to enhance the flavor and texture.

12 SERVINGS

10 bacon slices

1¾ cups yellow cornmeal

1¼ cups unbleached all purpose flour

¼ cup sugar

1 tablespoon baking powder

¾ teaspoon salt

½ teaspoon baking soda

6 tablespoons (¾ stick) chilled unsalted butter, cut into ½-inch pieces

1½ cups buttermilk

3 large eggs

1⅓ cups chopped green onions

1 8½- to 8¾-ounce can cream-style corn

Preheat oven to 400°F. Working in batches, cook bacon in heavy large skillet over medium heat until brown and crisp, turning occasionally, about 6 minutes per batch. Transfer bacon to paper towels and drain thoroughly. Crumble bacon into small pieces. Reserve 5 tablespoons bacon drippings.

Grease 9x9x2-inch baking pan with 1 tablespoon bacon drippings. Mix cornmeal, flour, sugar, baking powder, salt and baking soda in large bowl. Add chilled butter and rub in with fingertips until mixture resembles coarse meal. Whisk buttermilk, 3 eggs and remaining 4 tablespoons reserved bacon drippings in medium bowl to blend. Add buttermilk mixture to dry ingredients and stir until blended. Mix in chopped green onions, corn and crumbled bacon.

Transfer batter to prepared pan.

Bake corn bread until golden and tester inserted into center comes out clean, about 35 minutes. Cool corn bread in pan on rack. *(Can be prepared 8 hours ahead. Cover tightly with aluminum foil and let stand at room temperature.)* Cut corn bread into squares and serve.

BENNE SEED CHEDDAR CRISPS

Sesame seeds were brought to the colonies by West African slaves, who called them benne seeds. They were often used in biscuits and cookies. Meanwhile, varieties of cheddar cheese were being made by colonists in New England and New York; the cheese was popular in biscuit and cracker recipes. The two ingredients team up perfectly in these treats.

MAKES ABOUT 3 DOZEN

¼ cup sesame seeds

8 ounces grated sharp cheddar cheese (about 2 cups)

½ cup (1 stick) butter, room temperature

1 tablespoon Oriental sesame oil

1¼ cups all purpose flour

¼ teaspoon salt

⅛ teaspoon cayenne pepper

Stir sesame seeds in large skillet over medium heat until just golden, about 4 minutes. Transfer to bowl and cool.

Using electric mixer, beat cheese and butter in large bowl until blended. Slowly beat in oil. Mix in flour, salt, cayenne and 3 tablespoons sesame seeds. Gently knead on work surface until dough comes together. Shape dough into 10-inch-long log. Wrap in plastic and chill until firm, about 45 minutes. (*Can be made 2 weeks ahead. Wrap in heavy-duty foil and freeze. Defrost dough in refrigerator before continuing.*)

Preheat oven to 350°F. Line 2 baking sheets with foil. Slice cheese log into ¼-inch-thick rounds. Place rounds on baking sheets. Bake until crisp and light brown, about 18 minutes. Remove from oven; immediately sprinkle 1 tablespoon sesame seeds over crisps, patting gently to adhere. (*Can be made 1 day ahead. Cool completely. Store in airtight container. Before serving, rewarm in 350°F oven about 5 minutes.*)

A CRACKER OF A SNACK

Crackers are typically a good snack choice, especially when compared with fat-laden, high-calorie junk food. But most crackers don't have enough taste to satisfy hunger pains. The Seattle-based snack producer Partners has rolled out a new line of rich-tasting crackers that are as guilt-free as they are addictive. Wisecrackers have less sodium and fat than saltines or wheat crackers, but theflavors–like Roasted Garlic and Rosemary, Spicy Pepper Melange, and Original Sesame–will make even junk-food junkies reach for them first. Look for Wisecrackers in supermarkets.

Pasta

The humble but multifaceted Italian staple remains one of our most popular dishes, whether cooked at home or ordered at a restaurant. Many pastas make ideal sit-down first courses, such as Tagliatelle with Smoked Salmon Cream or Fettuccine with Sweet Pepper-Cayenne Sauce. Other dishes, particularly those based on bite-sized shapes like Fusilli with Porcini Puttanesca Sauce or Pumpkin Dumplings, may be neatly served and eaten as part of an appetizer buffet.

Seafood Sauces

Tagliatelle with Smoked Salmon Cream Sauce

A quick yet elegant pasta dish.

4 FIRST-COURSE SERVINGS

1 8-ounce bottle clam juice
1 cup whipping cream
¼ cup chopped fresh dill or
   2 teaspoons dried dillweed
1 teaspoon fresh lemon juice
12 ounces tagliatelle or linguine,
   freshly cooked
4 ounces smoked salmon, cut into
   thin strips

   Lemon wedges

Bring clam juice and cream to boil in heavy large skillet over high heat. Reduce heat and simmer until mixture thickens enough to coat spoon, whisking occasionally, about 10 minutes. Whisk in dill and lemon juice. Add tagliatelle and toss to coat. Remove skillet from heat. Add salmon and toss to combine. Season pasta to taste with salt and pepper.

   Divide pasta among 4 plates. Serve with lemon wedges.

Linguine with Shrimp and Sun-dried Tomato Sauce

4 SERVINGS

3 ounces sun-dried tomatoes
   (not oil-packed)

2 tablespoons (¼ stick) butter
1 medium onion, sliced
3 tablespoons all purpose flour
1½ cups bottled clam juice
1 cup half and half
½ pound Fontina cheese, grated
1 pound uncooked shrimp, peeled,
   deveined
¾ pound linguine, freshly cooked

Place tomatoes in bowl; add hot water to cover. Let stand until tomatoes soften, about 10 minutes. Drain; slice thinly.

   Melt butter in large pot over medium heat. Add onion; sauté until translucent, about 5 minutes. Add flour; stir 2 minutes. Add clam juice, half and half, cheese and tomatoes. Bring to boil, stirring frequently. Reduce heat to medium-low; simmer until sauce thickens and coats spoon, stirring occasionally, about 6 minutes. Add shrimp; simmer until just opaque in center, about 3 minutes. Add pasta and toss to coat. Season with salt and pepper.

Vegetable Sauces

PASTA WITH ROASTED VEGETABLES, TOMATOES AND BASIL

Great served warm or at room temperature.

6 TO 8 SERVINGS

Nonstick vegetable oil spray
2 red bell peppers, cut into
   ½-inch pieces
1 medium eggplant, unpeeled,
   cut into ½-inch pieces
1 large yellow crookneck squash,
   cut into ½-inch pieces
1½ cups ½-inch pieces peeled
   butternut squash
4 tablespoons olive oil

1 pound penne pasta

2 medium tomatoes, cored,
   seeded, diced

½ cup chopped fresh basil or
   1½ tablespoons dried
2 tablespoons balsamic vinegar
1 garlic clove, minced
½ cup grated Parmesan cheese

Preheat oven to 450°F. Spray large roasting pan with nonstick spray. Combine red bell peppers, eggplant, crookneck squash and butternut squash in prepared pan. Drizzle with 2 tablespoons olive oil; sprinkle with salt and pepper. Toss to coat. Roast until vegetables are tender and beginning to brown, stirring occasionally, about 25 minutes.

Meanwhile, cook pasta in large pot of boiling salted water until just tender but still firm to bite. Drain, reserving ½ cup cooking liquid.

Combine pasta, roasted vegetables, tomatoes and basil in large bowl. Add remaining 2 tablespoons oil, vinegar and garlic. Toss to combine. Season pasta to taste with salt and pepper, adding reserved cooking liquid by tablespoonfuls to moisten, if desired. Mound pasta on serving platter. Sprinkle with Parmesan cheese and serve.

PENNE WITH MUSHROOMS, TOMATOES AND BASIL

A quick and flavorful pasta.

4 SERVINGS

6 tablespoons olive oil
1 small onion, chopped
6 large garlic cloves, chopped
¾ pound mushrooms, thickly sliced
2 teaspoons chopped fresh
   rosemary or 1½ teaspoons dried
½ cup chopped fresh basil
⅔ cup dry white wine
1 14½- to 16-ounce can diced
   tomatoes
1 cup canned low-salt chicken broth

¾ pound penne, freshly cooked
  Grated Parmesan cheese

Heat oil in heavy large pot over medium-high heat. Add onion and garlic and sauté 1 minute. Add mushrooms, rosemary and ¼ cup basil. Sauté until onion and mushrooms are tender, about 8 minutes. Add wine. Boil until most of wine evaporates, about 3 minutes. Add tomatoes with their juices and broth. Boil until sauce thickens slightly, stirring occasionally, about 5 minutes. Add penne and remaining ¼ cup basil to pot. Toss pasta with sauce until well coated and heated through. Season to taste with salt and pepper. Serve, passing Parmesan cheese separately.

Pumpkin Dumplings

Remarkably easy and delicious dumplings that are similar to Italian gnocchi.

4 SIDE-DISH SERVINGS

½ cup canned solid pack pumpkin
1 large egg
½ teaspoon salt
⅛ teaspoon grated nutmeg
⅛ teaspoon (generous) baking
  powder
½ cup all purpose flour

3 tablespoons butter
½ cup grated Parmesan cheese

Bring large pot of salted water to boil. Whisk pumpkin, egg, salt, nutmeg and baking powder in large bowl to blend. Mix in flour (dough will be soft).

Dip ½-teaspoon measuring spoon into boiling water to moisten. Scoop up generous ½ teaspoon of dough and return spoon to water, allowing dough to drop. Working in 2 batches, repeat dropping ½ teaspoonfuls of dough into water, first dipping spoon into water to moisten each time. Boil dumplings until cooked through, about 10 minutes. Using slotted spoon, transfer to colander and drain.

Melt butter in heavy large skillet over medium heat. Add dumplings. Sauté until beginning to brown, about 8 minutes. Transfer dumplings to bowl. Sprinkle with cheese and serve.

FUSILLI WITH PORCINI PUTTANESCA SAUCE

Porcini mushrooms smooth out the intense flavors of this traditional sauce of tomatoes, olives, anchovies and capers. Although puttanesca sauce is typically served with penne or spaghetti, fusilli holds the sauce better.

4 SERVINGS

1⅓ cups hot water
 ½ ounce (about ¾ cup) dried
     porcini mushrooms*

 1 28-ounce can diced peeled
     tomatoes in juice
1¼ cups finely chopped onion
1½ tablespoons minced garlic
 12 Niçois olives,** pitted, chopped
 2 tablespoons tomato paste
1½ tablespoons drained capers
1½ tablespoons chopped anchovy
     fillets
 1 teaspoon dried oregano
 1 teaspoon dried basil
 ⅛ teaspoon dried crushed red pepper

 8 ounces fusilli pasta

Combine 1⅓ cups hot water and porcini in small bowl. Let stand until porcini are soft, about 25 minutes. Strain porcini, reserving liquid; discard sandy residue in bottom of bowl. Coarsely chop porcini.

Drain tomatoes, reserving juice. Bring juice to boil in large saucepan. Add onion and garlic. Reduce heat and simmer until onion is tender, about 15 minutes. Add porcini, reserved porcini liquid, tomatoes, olives and next 6 ingredients. Partially cover pot and simmer sauce until thickened slightly, about 30 minutes. Season with salt and pepper.

Cook pasta in large pot of boiling salted water until just tender but still firm to bite. Drain pasta. Return to pot. Add sauce to pasta. Toss to blend.

*Available at Italian markets, specialty foods stores and many supermarkets.

**Small brine-cured black olives, available at specialty foods stores and in some supermarkets nationwide.

FETTUCCINE WITH SWEET PEPPER-CAYENNE SAUCE

4 SERVINGS

 3 tablespoons butter
 2 large red bell peppers, cut into
     ¼-inch-thick strips
 3 garlic cloves, minced
 ¾ teaspoon cayenne pepper
 1 cup whipping cream
 ¾ cup canned low-salt chicken broth
 ¾ cup grated Parmesan cheese

 12 ounces fettuccine
 1 cup frozen green peas
 ½ cup chopped fresh basil

Melt butter in heavy large skillet over medium heat. Add bell peppers, garlic and cayenne; stir to blend. Cover skillet; cook until peppers are tender, stirring occasionally, about 7 minutes. Uncover; add cream and broth and simmer until liquid is slightly thickened, about 5 minutes. Stir in ½ cup Parmesan. Remove from heat.

Meanwhile, cook fettuccine in large pot of boiling salted water until just tender but still firm to bite. Add peas to pot. Drain. Return fettuccine and peas to pot. Add bell pepper mixture and basil; toss. Season with salt and pepper. Transfer to large bowl. Sprinkle with ¼ cup Parmesan.

Cheese Sauces

RIGATONI WITH GORGONZOLA CHEESE

8 SERVINGS

2½ tablespoons butter
 ½ cup fresh breadcrumbs
   (from French bread)

1¼ cups whole milk
 ½ cup whipping cream
 1 tablespoon all purpose flour
12 ounces Gorgonzola cheese, crumbled

 1 pound rigatoni or penne pasta
 ¼ cup grated Parmesan cheese

Preheat oven to 400°F. Butter 13x9x2-inch glass baking dish. Melt ½ tablespoon butter in small nonstick skillet over medium heat. Add breadcrumbs and stir until golden, about 4 minutes. Remove skillet from heat.

Bring milk and cream to simmer in medium saucepan. Remove from heat. Melt remaining 2 tablespoons butter in another medium saucepan over low heat. Add flour; stir 2 minutes. Whisk in milk mixture. Whisk until slightly thickened, about 4 minutes. Add Gorgonzola and whisk until cheese melts and sauce is almost smooth. Set aside.

Cook pasta in large pot of boiling salted water until just tender but still firm to bite. Drain. Return pasta to pot. Add Gorgonzola sauce to pasta and toss to coat. Season pasta to taste with salt and pepper. Transfer to prepared baking dish. Sprinkle with grated Parmesan cheese and breadcrumbs. Bake pasta until sauce bubbles, about 25 minutes. Let stand 5 minutes and serve.

GORGONZOLA

This world-famous veined cheese originally came from the town of the same name just east of Milan in the northern region of Lombardy. In times past, the village of Gorgonzola was a stop for herdsmen driving cattle between the Alps and the grassy plains above the Po Valley. Legend has it that the accumulation of herds in this one spot led to the creation of the cheese as a way of preserving all the milk they produced. But that was long ago; today, far more Gorgonzola is made in the neighboring region of Piedmont than in its birthplace.

There are actually two types of DOC Gorgonzola available. The younger cheese, called *Gorgonzola dolce,* is aged no more than three months, resulting in a smooth, creamy, almost runny paste. It is superb on crusty bread or unflavored crackers. Possibly better known to Americans is *Gorgonzola naturale* (also called *piccante*), which is cured for more than three months. This has a more compact paste and is pale ivory-white to alabaster in color. Both types have the characteristic blue-green veins running through them. *Penicillium glaucum* is added to the curd at the beginning of cheesemaking to create the flavorful mold. During the curing process, the cheese is regularly pierced with thick stainless steel or copper needles to let air into the interior and encourage the mold to grow and spread throughout the cheese, forming the veins.

In buying Gorgonzola dolce, look for cheese that has a glistening, buttery-smooth paste the color of fresh cream and that is well marked with veining. Because it has been aged longer, Gorgonzola naturale is drier than the dolce, is often alabaster white in color, and has decidedly blue veins. With either variety, avoid any cheese that shows pink or yellow streaks in the interior, which indicate that it is past its prime.

LINGUINE WITH PEARS AND GORGONZOLA CHEESE

Pears and Gorgonzola are a classic combination in Italy; here they team up in a unique pasta recipe. To make this intriguing dish even heartier, toss in some diced ham or cooked chicken.

8 APPETIZER SERVINGS

¼ cup (½ stick) butter
4 firm pears (about 2 pounds),
   peeled, cored, sliced into
   ⅓-inch-thick strips

1 tablespoon (scant) chopped fresh
   rosemary or 1½ teaspoons dried
1 cup canned low-salt chicken broth
4 ounces Gorgonzola cheese,
   crumbled
¾ cup grated Parmesan cheese
½ cup whipping cream
¾ pound linguine, freshly cooked
⅓ cup chopped pecans, toasted

Melt butter in heavy large skillet over medium-high heat. Add pears and sauté until tender and beginning to brown but not soft, about 8 minutes. Using slotted spoon, carefully transfer pears to bowl.

Add rosemary to same skillet and stir until fragrant, about 1 minute. Add broth, Gorgonzola cheese, ½ cup Parmesan cheese and cream. Simmer until sauce thickens enough to coat spoon, whisking occasionally, about 6 minutes. Return pears and any accumulated juices to sauce. (*Can be made 2 hours ahead. Let stand at room temperature. Bring to simmer before continuing.*)

Add linguine and pecans to sauce. Toss over medium-low heat until sauce coats pasta, about 3 minutes. Season to taste with salt and pepper. Transfer to large bowl. Sprinkle with remaining ¼ cup Parmesan cheese.

PASTA WITH TOMATOES, MOZZARELLA AND BASIL

4 SERVINGS

1½ pounds plum tomatoes, seeded,
   coarsely chopped
8 ounces fresh mozzarella cheese,
   cut into 1x½-inch strips
3 tablespoons extra-virgin olive oil
2 teaspoons red wine vinegar
½ cup chopped fresh basil

12 ounces penne pasta

Mix tomatoes, mozzarella, oil and vinegar in medium bowl. Season with salt and pepper. Let stand 1 hour at room temperature. Mix in basil.

Cook pasta in large pot of boiling salted water until just tender but still firm to bite. Drain. Return pasta to pot. Add tomato mixture and toss gently to blend. Season with salt and pepper and serve.

KEEPING PASTA LIGHT *AND* SATISFYING

On its own, pasta is very low in fat and is a healthful source of complex carbohydrates. However, when it gets served with rich butter or cream sauces, or covered in cheese, or teamed with sausage or bacon, the fat level starts to climb fast. Here are a few tips on how to keep your pasta dishes rich-tasting and satisfying without being weighed down with fat.

Vegetables. Use them generously. Any one (or combination of a few) will work, but the truly substantial ones, like cauliflower, broccoli and cabbage, will make it seem as if you're getting more.

Canned tomatoes. Of course, most tomato-based sauces are much better, health-wise, than butter and cream sauces. You can take that notion to the next level by using juices from the canned tomatoes (or try chicken broth) instead of oil or butter to cook the vegetables. Be sure to use a nonstick pan.

Pasta shape. Choose hefty, dense pasta shapes like fusilli, penne, *farfalle* or shells rather than the more delicate strands, such as linguine, spaghetti or *capellini*. The bulkier shapes look like more food on your plate, and they hold the sauce better.

High-flavor ingredients. A little bit of these items goes a long way. Since you don't need much, you won't be loading up on fat and calories; plus, their assertiveness means you don't need to add fat for taste. Think of roasted bell peppers, anchovies, olives and smoked salmon. Of course, ingredients like capers, garlic, herbs, citrus zest and red pepper flakes are always good additions to pasta.

High-flavor cheese. See above for the philosophy. Most people agree that pasta just isn't pasta without some cheese. By selecting the more intense ones, such as Parmesan, Romano, *ricotta salata*, feta or any blue, you can get away with using just a little for a lot of flavor.

Pureed ingredients. These can help thicken the texture of a sauce without increasing the fat too much. Items that work especially well include pureed canned white beans, cooked carrots, canned tomatoes, olives, anchovies and roasted bell peppers.

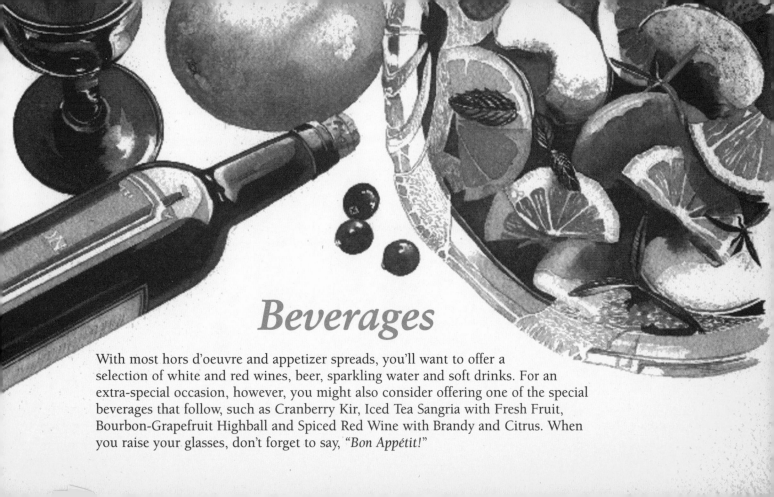

Beverages

With most hors d'oeuvre and appetizer spreads, you'll want to offer a selection of white and red wines, beer, sparkling water and soft drinks. For an extra-special occasion, however, you might also consider offering one of the special beverages that follow, such as Cranberry Kir, Iced Tea Sangria with Fresh Fruit, Bourbon-Grapefruit Highball and Spiced Red Wine with Brandy and Citrus. When you raise your glasses, don't forget to say, *"Bon Appétit!"*

Wines

Iced Tea Sangria with Fresh Fruit

This is a refreshing drink for the cocktail hour. Use any kind of black tea you like; fruit-flavored ones are particularly nice.

4 SERVINGS

4 cups water
2 tea bags
4 to 5 tablespoons sugar

1 peach or apple, peeled, pitted or seeded, chopped
4 large strawberries, hulled, halved
1 orange, all peel and white pith removed, cut into ¾-inch pieces
1 cup dry red wine
    Ice cubes

Bring water to boil in medium saucepan. Remove from heat. Add tea bags; steep 3 minutes. Remove tea bags; pour tea into pitcher. Add sugar to taste and stir until sugar dissolves. Cool. (*Can be made 1 day ahead. Cover and refrigerate.*)

Mix fruit in bowl. Divide among four 16-ounce glasses. Pour ¼ cup wine, then 1 cup tea into each glass. Fill glasses with ice cubes and serve.

Mulled Madeira

Madeira is combined with Cointreau, honey and spices in a simple English-inspired hot drink for the holidays.

6 SERVINGS

4 cups Madeira
6 tablespoons honey
2 tablespoons fresh lemon juice
8 3-inch-long, ½-inch-wide orange peel strips (orange part only)
6 whole cloves
1 cinnamon stick, broken in half
½ cup Cointreau or other orange liqueur

Combine first 6 ingredients in heavy large saucepan. Bring almost to simmer over medium heat. Reduce heat to low and cook wine mixture 10 minutes to allow flavors to blend (do not simmer). Add Cointreau and stir until heated through. Ladle into heat-proof glasses or mugs, leaving orange peel and spices in pan. Serve punch warm.

SPICY-SMOKY PEANUTS

These roasted peanuts have a rich, smoky flavor that makes them a good accompaniment to cocktails.

MAKES 2 CUPS

2 cups husked shelled raw Spanish peanuts (about 10 ounces)
4 teaspoons Worcestershire sauce
1 tablespoon liquid smoke flavoring*

2 tablespoons (¼ stick) butter
2 teaspoons distilled white vinegar
2 teaspoons hot pepper sauce (such as Tabasco)
¾ teaspoon salt
⅛ teaspoon cayenne pepper

Line jelly roll pan with foil. Toss peanuts, Worcestershire sauce and liquid smoke in pan. Let marinate at room temperature, stirring occasionally, about 30 minutes.

Position rack in center of oven and preheat to 325°F. Melt butter in heavy large skillet over medium-low heat. Cool slightly. Stir in vinegar, hot pepper sauce, salt and cayenne. Return skillet to heat. Scrape in nuts and marinade. Stir to coat nuts, about 30 seconds. Return nut mixture to jelly roll pan. Bake until deep golden brown, stirring occasionally, about 20 minutes. Transfer pan to rack and cool. Let stand uncovered 6 hours to dry. (*Can be made 1 week ahead. Store nuts in airtight container at room temperature.*)

*A smoke-flavored liquid seasoning available at specialty foods stores and at many supermarkets.

CRANBERRY KIR

Cranberries are cultivated in Canada, and tradition there calls for hosts to make a punch for Christmas guests. Here, the crop and the custom merge in a delightful champagne cocktail, which takes a French turn with the addition of crème de cassis.

12 SERVINGS

1½ cups chilled cranberry juice
¾ cup crème de cassis (black currant-flavored liqueur)
1 750-ml bottle chilled dry champagne or sparkling wine

Place 2 tablespoons cranberry juice and 1 tablespoon crème de cassis in each of 12 champagne flutes. Pour ¼ cup champagne into each and serve.

Spiced Red Wine with Brandy and Citrus

The French often serve flavored wine as an aperitif. This one has a base of red wine infused with orange, lemon, vanilla and cloves; it is later mixed with raspberry brandy and sugar. The drink is best at cool room temperature, accompanied by nibbles such as olives, almonds and crudités. It also makes an excellent Christmas present–just double or triple the recipe, and pour the drink into pretty bottles. Be sure to begin the process at least three weeks before you plan to have the wine or give it as a gift.

MAKES 3 CUPS

1 orange, sliced
½ lemon, sliced
1 vanilla bean
   Peel from 1 orange (orange part only, removed with vegetable peeler)
6 whole cloves
1 750-ml bottle dry red wine (such as Côtes du Rhône or Merlot)
½ cup framboise eau-de-vie (clear raspberry brandy) or brandy
6 tablespoons sugar

Combine sliced orange and lemon, vanilla bean, orange peel and cloves in large glass jar. Pour wine over. Cover and place in cool dark area for 2 weeks.

Strain wine through several layers of cheesecloth into 4-cup measuring cup. Discard solids in cheesecloth. Add framboise and sugar to wine; stir until sugar dissolves. Pour mixture into wine bottle or decorative bottle. Cork bottle and place in cool dark area for at least 1 week. (*Can be made 6 weeks ahead. Store in cool dark area.*) Serve in small wineglasses.

Cocktails & Punches

Bourbon-Grapefruit Highball

2 SERVINGS

Ice cubes
6 tablespoons bourbon
10 dashes angostura bitters
1½ cups grapefruit soda

Fill two 14- to 16-ounce glasses with ice. Divide bourbon and bitters, then soda between glasses. Stir to blend.

MARTINI SIGHTINGS

"America's lethal weapon" is how Nikita Khrushchev once described the Martini, and this "weapon" is once again being brandished all over America–albeit in unusual ways. Here are a few places that have found the recipe for success (or should that be excess?). Cheers!

Atlanta: The Martini Club offers 54 varieties of the cocktail, among them China Blue, with a dash of Canton ginger liqueur, and the Garden Martini, which contains olive juice and a pickled asparagus spear.

Boston: At the Parish Cafe, favorites include Doebeli's Delicious, with Godiva Liqueur, and the Burlington Manhattan, sweetened with maple syrup.

Cincinnati: Trio's most popular renditions are Ray's Peppertini, featuring Absolut Peppar, and the French Kiss, which contains Chambord.

Minneapolis: Two that stir up orders at The Lounge are the Lemon Drop, with Cointreau and 7UP, and the Lounge Lizard, which calls for Midori.

St. Louis: Martinis at Tangerine are named after members of the Rat Pack. Their big hits are the "nutty" MacLaine, with Absolut and amaretto, and the Lawford, which is actually a classic gimlet made with Beefeater gin.

Spiced Rum and Tea Punch

This German drink, called Grossmutters Punsch (Grandmother's Punch), is usually enjoyed warm at midnight on Christmas Eve. It can also be served as a refreshing chilled drink. For a festive touch, add a cinnamon stick to each glass.

6 SERVINGS

2¼ cups water
⅓ cup honey
¼ cup (packed) golden brown sugar
2 tablespoons chopped peeled
  fresh ginger
16 whole cloves
16 whole allspice
1 vanilla bean, chopped
1 tea bag (preferably Earl Grey)
1 750-ml bottle dry red wine
¼ cup dark rum

Crushed ice (if serving punch chilled)

Combine water, honey, sugar, ginger, cloves, allspice and vanilla bean in heavy large saucepan. Bring mixture to boil over medium-high heat, stirring until honey and sugar dissolve. Boil 5 minutes. Remove from heat. Add tea bag; let steep 5 minutes. Strain syrup into bowl. Add wine and rum. If serving cold, refrigerate until chilled. (*Can be prepared 1 day ahead. Cover and refrigerate.*)

If serving cold, fill 6 glasses with crushed ice. Ladle punch into glasses. If serving hot, bring to simmer in medium saucepan. Pour punch into cups.

A COCKTAIL BOOM

Trade whiskey is going great guns at The Fort restaurant outside of Denver. This potent concoction of bourbon, red chili pepper, tobacco teas and a hefty pinch of black gunpowder (don't try this at home) was prized in the last century by some Native Americans, who traded furs for the brew.

"It tastes much better than pure bourbon," claims Fort owner Sam Arnold. "At least, that's what the Indians thought. There's this story about an Indian who was given really good whiskey, but he threatened to scalp the guy unless he got him the spicy stuff he was used to." No wonder it was called the Wild West.

Index

Acknowledgements & Credits

Recipes supplied by:

B.A. Test Kitchen
Lynda Hotch Balslev
Mary Barber
Nancy Verde Barr
Cherryl & Tom Barthiaume
Lena Cederham Birnbaum
Jennifer Braccia
Leslie Vaughn Burckard
Sarah & Rives Castleman
Sara Corpening
Lane Crowther
Nancy Currey
Janet Hazen De Jesus

Lorenza de'Medici
Lori & Jean Louis De Mori
Kathy & Robert Du Grenier
Sheila Eaton
Janet Fletcher
Jim Fobel
Millie Pozzo Froeb
Margaret & Stephen Gadient
Bradford & Jayne Gill
Sophie Grigson
Kathy Gunst
Judith Hausman
Mily Hernandez
Carl Hittinger
Nancy Harmon Jenkins

Karen Kaplan
Jeanne Thiel Kelley
Kristine Kidd
Jennifer Kirkgaard
Daveena Limonick
James H. Magruder
Michael McLaughlin
Crystal & Bob Moll
Selma Brown Morrow
Gina & Rich Mortillaro
Marcia Munson
Scott Peacock
Mary V. Petrara
Giuseppe Pistone
Sarah Smith Poole

Mimi Rippee
Claudia Roden
Douglas Rodriguez
Betty Rosbottom
Nicole Routhier
Lina Selvaggio
Martha Rose Shulman
Melissa & Tom Swartwout
Karen Turner
Karen & Tom Uhlmann
Joanne Weir
Lisa A. Wilson
Terri Pischoff Wuerthner
Mayda Yaghsezian

Text:
Laurie Glenn Buckle
Anthony Head
Katie O'Kennedy
Tanya Wenman Steel

Concept:
Tamra Febesh
Barbra Schnur
Linda Alexander

*Editorial development and
original writing:*
Norman Kolpas

Graphic Design:
Sandy Douglas

Illustrations:
Michelle Burchard

Index:
Barbara Wurf

Proofreader:
Katie Goldman

Rights and permissions:
Sybil Shimazu Neubauer

Typography:
TeleText Typography, Inc.